"What a needed message! I was once a  daddy, wishing I could know that he love to be rejected, abandoned, and forgot and I love that Kia so honestly and bib the arms of our Father, who will never le̶a̶v̶e̶ ̶o̶r̶ ̶f̶o̶r̶g̶e̶t̶ ̶u̶s̶. This resource will help so many!"

Lysa TerKeurst, #1 *New York Times* bestselling author
and president of Proverbs 31 Ministries

"There's something remarkable about the way a person's pain can be transformed into purpose. In *Overcoming Father Wounds*, Kia Stephens speaks from the faded scars of her own story and is a compassionate guide to all who carry father wounds of their own. Kia's book is both personal testimony and practical treatise; her words offer hope and healing. Words that help us discover the power of a heavenly Father's love."

Jo Saxton, leadership coach and author of *Ready to Rise*

"Kia has given us a powerful, gospel-soaked healing balm for everyone who knows the pain of father wounds. In *Overcoming Father Wounds*, she helps us identify them, heal from them, and shift our mindset to hope and health. This is a must-read!"

Alli Worthington, author, speaker, and founder
of The Coach School

"This book is going to help so many women—coming from complicated relationships with fathers to deeply painful ones. Even Daddy's girls like me didn't escape unintentional wounding. You'll be highlighting this one and buying a copy for a friend."

Lisa Whittle, bestselling author of *The Hard Good*,
Bible teacher, and podcast host

"Kia Stephens's voice is one that is needed now. She writes with compassion, wisdom, and vulnerability, leading women into the tender places of their own hearts. With deep insight, Kia takes the reader's hand and walks her into the truth—you can face the wounds you received, in the light of a loving Father who is better than you dared to hope. Healing is available. Read this book and Kia will show you the way."

Stasi Eldredge, *New York Times* bestselling coauthor of *Captivating*

"There are few relationships that play as great a role in our lives as the one we have with our father. For many, this relationship was imperfect. At times we may have found ourselves left wanting more than what our earthly fathers could give, leaving us feeling disappointed and seeking fulfillment in unhealthy ways. In *Overcoming Father Wounds*, Kia Stephens transparently shares her experiences navigating this territory of the soul and spirit. She uncovers the wounded areas in need of restoration and gives practical next steps in the healing journey. In this book, Kia extends an invitation to go beyond the pain of your father wounds to experience the joy of intimately knowing Father God."

Dr. Saundra Dalton-Smith, physician, author, and host of *I Choose My Best Life* podcast

"Wounds have the power to break us or lead us to healing, even the ones caused by the men who brought us into this world. In *Overcoming Father Wounds*, Kia not only gifts us with the vulnerability of her story about healing her own father wounds (with her faith in tow), but she shows us wounded sisters how to do it for ourselves too. What a gift these words are."

Toni J. Collier, author, speaker, and founder of Broken Crayons Still Color

"If you find that your heart holds a pinch when you think of your earthly father—or the absent father you never knew—this helpful and biblical resource will become a balm for your hurting soul. In *Overcoming Father Wounds*, Kia Stephens helps us relinquish the perpetual pains from our past and lean into the love of our heavenly Father like never before. Highly recommended for all daughters who desperately need to know they are greatly treasured, earnestly wanted, and eternally loved."

Karen Ehman, speaker and *New York Times* bestselling author of eighteen books, including *Settle My Soul*

"When hurts or beliefs distort our view of God, He is deeply invested in healing that place. Father wounds may be some of the most damaging of all, since they directly affect the way we perceive our heavenly Father. In *Overcoming Father Wounds*, God has used Kia Stephens to empathetically and practically point us toward the true, healing nature of Abba Father, the One who wants to have a close, mutual relationship with us."

Amy Carroll, speaker and author of *Breaking Up with Perfect* and *Exhale*

"Too many women live with unhealed hurts from their fathers. Kia Stephens was one of them. In *Overcoming Father Wounds*, she vulnerably unpacks her story and speaks out of the overflow of her restored heart after facing the pain of rejection and abandonment from her biological father. She doesn't give pat answers. Instead, she comes alongside as a friend and mentor, taking us by the hand, while modeling what it looks like to go through the process of surrender and forgiveness to move toward freedom and transformation. Thank you, Kia, for your courageous example that invites us to do the same."

Dr. Michelle Watson Canfield, LPC, author of *Let's Talk* and radio/podcast host of *The Dad Whisperer*

"I love how Kia peels back the complicated layers of this tender topic with tremendous wisdom, scriptural soundness, and raw vulnerability. Rather than just tell her story, Kia casts a powerful vision for God's deeper work within a woman's father wound, and she provides powerful and practical steps for any woman open to God's healing process. For every woman who needs to take this redemptive journey, Kia's book serves as a wise, godly, and compassionate guide each step of the way."

Barb Roose, speaker and author of numerous books
and Bible studies, including *Breakthrough*

"In *Overcoming Father Wounds*, Kia gives real and practical hope to the woman who questions if she's too broken to ever live whole. By authentically sharing her own story of father wounds, Kia courageously clears the path for women familiar with this pain to find their way to true healing. I have worked in vocational Christian ministry over three decades and have mentored and walked with women of all ages. The vast majority of these women have unhealthy relationships with their earthly fathers. The unprocessed emotions lead to challenges relationally and spiritually. In her powerful book, Kia Stephens openly shares from her own life and offers insights, Bible teaching, and practical help for women to heal and walk in freedom."

Vivian Mabuni, speaker, author of *Open Hands, Willing Feet*,
and founder and podcast host of *Someday Is Here*

"I admire the transparency Kia uses to point the reader into the loving arms of the Perfect Father who sees, knows, pursues, and proudly calls His girls by the best name . . . 'daughter.'"

Tarah-Lynn Saint-Elien, author of *Claim Your Crown*
and *Love Letters from the King*

"Kia is a brave new voice, reaching out personally to an audience of women wading through life with father wounds. Drawing deeply on her own experience, Kia ushers readers through Scripture into personal reflection with the goal of leading them to the heavenly Father's arms. This book is so needed today. I'm eager to share it with friends."

Dorina Lazo Gilmore-Young, author, speaker,
and podcaster at *Eat Pray Run*

"What powerful hope to anyone carrying the ache of father wounds! In *Overcoming Father Wounds*, Kia shows how to exchange deep scars from an earthly father for the deeper love of our heavenly Father. Kia shares vulnerably and transparently about the childhood wounds she carried into adulthood, while also walking through the paths of grief, forgiveness, and healing God has done in her. Through practical, biblical steps and her own experience, Kia unfolds how to let go of hurt and expectations, honestly find God as Father to the fatherless, and become healthy and whole."

Lisa Appelo, speaker and author of *Life Can Be Good Again*

"Implementing a conservative, biblical model for healing the devastation of fatherlessness, Kia Stephens clears the path for those behind her. Don't rush through this book. By taking time to engage with the reflection questions, you'll swap your father wounds for the extravagant love of God the Father."

Anna LeBaron, author of *The Polygamist's Daughter*

"Father wounds. So many of us have them and have never identified them as such. In this beautiful resource, Kia Stephens helps us go to Father God for the healing we need, walking with us as we do the hard work leading to the wholeness we long for."

Lynn Cowell, speaker and author of the Bible studies *Fearless Women of the Bible* and *Esther*

"With the grace of a friend and the love of a sister, Kia reminds women that overcoming father wounds is possible. For any woman who wants to know how, Kia can show you the way."

Christina Patterson, founder and president, Beloved Women, Inc.

"Kia is the sister you've always wanted. The one who makes you laugh, empathizes with your issues, but looks you straight in the face and encourages you to keep moving forward. She writes with piercing clarity and a rhythmic authenticity that left me pondering the text long after I closed the book. Her words shine a light on the areas many of us with aching hearts haven't known how to give voice to. *Overcoming Father Wounds* reveals the hidden hurts and residual issues of our ailment, but with unflinching hope anchored in the Word of God, our sister reminds us that our healing and worth is truly found in the One who will never fail us."

Jenny Erlingsson, author and speaker, Milk & Honey Women

"Be prepared to be tenderly pried open by Kia Stephens's *Overcoming Father Wounds*. I heard myself on the pages, 'It's complicated.' I thought describing my relationship with my own father in those words along with its complex explanation and emotions were mine alone to bear. Kia's book revealed a diagnosis I didn't know I had and provided the language and community I had been unknowingly yearning for. Her words were both confronting and comforting in ways I did not know my heart and identity needed. I felt seen, I felt safe, and I felt whole."

Nicole O. Salmon, The Purpose Coach, Nicole O. Salmon Ministries

OVERCOMING
FATHER
WOUNDS

OVERCOMING FATHER WOUNDS

EXCHANGING YOUR PAIN FOR GOD'S PERFECT LOVE

KIA STEPHENS

Revell

a division of Baker Publishing Group
Grand Rapids, Michigan

Published by Revell
a division of Baker Publishing Group
PO Box 6287, Grand Rapids, MI 49516-6287
www.revellbooks.com

Printed in the United States of America

Library of Congress Cataloging-in-Publication Data
Names: Stephens, Kia, 1979– author.
Title: Overcoming father wounds : exchanging your pain for God's perfect love / Kia Stephens.
Description: Grand Rapids, MI : Revell, a division of Baker Publishing Group, [2023]
Identifiers: LCCN 2022014421 | ISBN 9780800740924 (paperback) | ISBN 9780800742843 (casebound) | ISBN 9781493439843 (ebook)
Subjects: LCSH: Abused women—Religious life. | Adult child sexual abuse victims—Religious life. | Christian women—Religious life. | Fathers and daughters. | Incest victims—Religious life.
Classification: LCC BV4596.A2 S74 2022 | DDC 261.8/3272—dc23/eng/20220801
LC record available at https://lccn.loc.gov/2022014421

The author is represented by the literary agency of Embolden Media Group, LLC.

Baker Publishing Group publications use paper produced from sustainable forestry practices and post-consumer waste whenever possible.

23   24   25   26   27   28   29   7   6   5   4   3   2   1

I dedicate this book to you. Our stories are different, but our ache is the same. If you have ever felt unloved, unwanted, unimportant, or wounded by your father, this book has been crafted with you in mind. It is my sincerest prayer that God fills and overflows every father-shaped vacuum in your soul. May you complete the pages of this book knowing that you are

Loved.

Wanted.

Valued.

Important.

Beautiful.

Precious.

Cherished.

Healed.

& Fathered.

CONTENTS

1

SOUNDING THE ALARM

The word *father* is enough to sucker-punch you without warning. It's a six-letter doozy loaded with connotations, good and bad. Immediately, it conjures up a series of spliced-together childhood memories of us and our fathers. And sometimes just us.

Like Pavlov's dog salivating at the sound of a bell, our bodies have an internal response to the mere utterance of the word. We may experience a tinge of disappointment or a surge of anger. We may even find ourselves encased within indifference (which is still a response). With little to no effort, we remember something about the man who gave us life, even if it is his absence.

And sometimes, that word leads us to this thought: *I wish I had a different father*. I'm convinced we say this in our minds more times than we'd like to admit. Nestled in that gray matter between our ears lie thoughts no one else is privy to: a perfectly crafted comeback, our opinion of the well-meaning but out-of-line church lady, and a few beliefs about the greenness of our grass.

This isn't to be confused with literal grass, rooted in dirt and fleecing the lawns of golf courses like a thick, fluffy blanket. I'm talking about figurative grass, composed of all that we are. It's the stuff that separates us from everyone else—family makeup, socioeconomic status, and experiences or the lack thereof.

Sometimes when we stand on our tippy-toes and look over the picket fence dividing our yard from our neighbor's, the hue of their grass looks greener. We see their well-manicured yard filled with plush green blades, only to turn, firmly place both feet on the ground, and stare back at our own grass.

Now, with acute clarity, we see the patches of tan and scrawny turf scattered throughout our lawn. We notice the place where grass doesn't exist at all. It is here discontentment sets in as we long to have the yard of our neighbors.

I have compared my grass with unassuming neighbors' enough to know that this type of displeasure doesn't play fair. It reaches to the tender-to-the-touch areas of our lives, teetering over into circumstances completely beyond our control, like our family. Before we know it, we're entertaining thoughts of what our life would've been like if we had an alternative upbringing: a two-parent household or a more engaged father.

We question what would've been different had our father been there to teach us how to ride a bike, attend our volleyball games, interrogate dates, struggle through the sex talk, and tell us we were pretty. In the secrecy of our inner thoughts, we imagine a father who stayed, was sober, lived a long life, never went to prison, never knew addictions, and loved only our mother all his days.

What would've been a distinctive and noticeable difference in us had we grown up with a different father? Would we be the same woman or an enhanced version of ourselves? More whole? More secure? More at peace? Here in the tangled labyrinth of our minds, we begin to contemplate the impossible: having a different father.

This, however, is not an option. We don't have the luxury of exchanging our father for a kinder or more attentive one. Our patch of grass, no matter the condition, is still ours. As a result, our father's attributes, good or bad, are embedded in the fabric of who he is. And although it's possible for people to change, we can't make our father who we want him to be. Every father-wounded daughter eventually faces the reality that she will not get a different dad.

> **Although it's possible for people to change, we can't make our father who we want him to be.**

This is why, although we've never met, there is a part of me that knows a part of you intimately. We are sisters bonded together by a wound we incurred when we were most vulnerable. We are a vast multi-ethnic society of women.

Extending beyond class and race, father wounds do not discriminate. They impact women everywhere. For a myriad of reasons, women have experienced wounds from their fathers. The vastness of this epidemic prompted me to write for women with these wounds.

A Sorority of the Wounded

"I'm going to start a blog for women who grew up without their fathers," I announced on separate occasions. Women responded first with their body language—widened eyes, turned heads, and a barely audible "Hmm," which all signaled to me they had a wound too. Then they spoke, confirming my suspicion.

"I just met my dad two weeks ago."
"I don't know who my father is."
"My daddy was an alcoholic."
"I heard my father call my mother a heifer."
"My dad introduced me as his boy."

Whether I was in the salon, on a playdate with my kids, or at work, women had something to say about their father-daughter relationships or lack thereof. Without hesitation, they recounted the memories (often painful) and words of their biological fathers.

Every woman seemed to have her father-daughter story filed in an easily accessible compartment ready to retrieve on cue. They divulged this information as if it were an uncomplicated sharing of facts.

Stoically, and with ease, they communicated painfully difficult truths about their fathers. Truths that, for many of them, drastically altered the trajectory of their lives. I understood their immediate and straightforward responses; I've given them too. Out of necessity, I meticulously crafted one-liners that quickly described the painful and difficult realities of my father-daughter story.

"My mom and dad got a divorce when I was a baby" and "I didn't grow up with my father" were staples I used in conversation. These were necessary survival must-haves that kept my emotions at bay. I attempted to articulate my raw truth in a way that would keep me from getting emotional in public. Thus, the hearer wouldn't feel the need to offer a kind but insufficient response. At all costs, I wanted to avoid the awkward silence that gut-honest truth elicits. Collectively, father-wounded women have learned that the average person either can't handle the realities of our stories or simply doesn't want to.

Denna D. Babul, a registered nurse and coauthor of the book *The Fatherless Daughter Project*, describes the motivation behind these matter-of-fact replies:

> Each time someone asks about your father, you probably have a brief story that you have kneaded and molded into a form that you can handle—and that others can handle —as you pushed through the significant years of your life without the security of a father–daughter bond. We need to protect our histories and our hearts from being hurt again in the retelling of what happened to our fathers. At the same time, we have felt compelled to protect those who are asking for an answer that might make them uncomfortable. We can become wary over time of the need to take care of someone after we have spilled a painful answer onto his lap, so we reshape the story and try out different versions to find one that works.[1]

Over time, survival instincts have taught us how to cope: by divorcing ourselves from emotional trauma in order to function. As a result, we craft our responses like injured soldiers headed back out to the battlefield. After all, life doesn't stop for the wounded—especially when the wounds can't be seen.

For more than six years I've been writing online about father wounds, and this intimate cyber conversation is still going strong, with voices continuously adding to the dialogue. During this time, we've exchanged "Me Toos" through blog posts and social media pictures, cried tears, revealed scars, and traded our stoicism for vulnerability. We've created a safe place amid the unsafe and very public domain of the internet.

It is in this conversation that I have grown, healed, taken risks, and discovered more about who I am, while simultaneously learning about the multi-ethnic society I'm writing for. From the beginning of my blogging journey, I've tried to make my writing an even exchange. I wanted readers to feel like my blog was a safe place, so I bared my soul first. With every blog post, I took the scary plunge into the vulnerability pool on their behalf. In fact, when I ventured onto the blogging scene, I told a good friend of mine, "I feel like I'm walking down Peachtree Street butt naked." There's no way to discuss father wounds without tackling a few of my biggest hurdles: self-esteem, relationships with men (Help me, Jesus!), and insecurities.

I knew that if I wanted to talk about exchanging father wounds for the love of God the Father, I was going to have to bring all of myself to the task. I would have to share my unfiltered truth. A blog about father wounds required me to be brutally honest about my flaws, faults, and issues.

This is why I felt completely bare on the internet when I pressed Publish on my very first blog post. Truth be told, it was probably just my mama reading in the beginning, but vulnerability is attractive. Like sugar water to a colony of ants, vulnerability draws women of every demographic and compels them to say, "Me too."

As women with father wounds began to visit the blog, they emailed me their stories, which were painful and difficult to digest but not surprising.

The women confirmed what I instinctively knew: father wounds were impacting women and they were suffering in silence. This fact birthed in me a desire to quantify what I knew anecdotally. To substantiate this reality, I needed to depend on my least favorite subject: math. I knew there was tremendous value in being able to quantify the scope of the problem.

A Sobering Survey

As a result, I decided to add a running survey to my blog and began to accumulate data from every woman who was willing to share it.

Initially, I checked the data weekly, because in my researcher mode the information was fascinating to me. But the more and more I checked the data, the more I was reminded that I wasn't just looking at numbers on a page. Each number represented a woman with a painful father wound.

I was looking at real women, each of whom had deep-seated emotions attached to every answer. As the number of survey respondents increased, it lodged a mammoth-sized weight in my heart. I was grieved for the number of women who'd been impacted by this issue, and it further solidified my resolve to do something about it.

To date, 925 women have completed the survey. That number is staggering, considering 99% of them admit to having father wounds. The ages of the women range from 18 to 75 and older. Their relationship status varies, although 47.8% of them are married.

When asked whether they considered themself a fatherless daughter, 58.1% said yes and 28.8% said no. In response to this question, there were several reasons why women didn't choose either yes or no. Some women identified God as their father, others said their father was deceased, and some said their father was in their life, but they didn't have a great relationship with him.

When asked about their upbringing, 66.4% said they were not fathered growing up. Twenty-nine percent of survey respondents indicated their father was not fathered growing up, and 28.9% said their mother was not fathered. Of the survey respondents, 17.2% of them are raising kids without fathers. This data revealed how the circumstance of parents with father wounds may predispose their kids to growing up without a father as well.

I also asked the survey respondents the cause of their father's absence. Twenty-nine percent of women grew up in divorced households, 26% experienced abandonment, 24% had a father who was addicted to either drugs or alcohol or both, and 9% lost their father due to death. Additionally, 44% of the women who completed the survey said their father was physically present but emotionally absent.

In response to the type of father women had, 32% said they grew up with an authoritarian father, 26% said their father was abusive, 35% indicated their father was distant or passive, and 38% said their father was absent. I also discovered 42.9% of women had experienced verbal abuse and 7% knew sexual abuse at the hands of their father. When asked about the status of the current relationship with their father, 34% said they had a deceased father, 23% said they had no relationship with their father at all, and the remaining women described their relationship as either close, somewhat close, distant, or inconsistent.

The most devastating data came from a question I wrestled with for most of my adult life. Toward the end of the survey, I asked the women if they'd been able to heal from the hurts in their father-daughter relationship. Of the survey respondents, 43.8% said they had not.

This percentage broke my heart. There were women among the survey respondents who had suffered for their entire lives—some of them possibly accepting the lie that they could never heal. The overwhelming majority of women were filling out the survey not because they particularly liked surveys. I wasn't offering them a gift card or entering their name into a giveaway. They freely took my survey because they were looking for something to help them heal.

Displayed through bar graphs and pie charts, their desperation leaped off the computer screen and tugged at the core of my heart. Increasingly, this data became more sobering to me. Each percentage represented a group of women with lives that had been devastated by father wounds. It was alarming and overwhelming at the same time.

Why aren't more people talking about this? I asked myself. *Why aren't there easily accessible support groups and counselors on hand? Where is the church? Why hasn't someone sounded the alarm?*

This data was cause for concern, at least for me. It represented more than just numbers. These were the women I was writing for. These were the women I was called to encourage. These were the women who were just like me.

This is why, without ever meeting you, I can say with confidence, "I understand." There is no need for you to explain or say, "It's complicated." I get it. I too have experienced an ache for the love of my father. I know the gnawing feeling of rejection that hijacks a woman's thoughts and influences what she tells herself when no one's looking. I know the suffocating fear that snuffs out dreams like a hit man. I know the ambition that drives you to achieve more in order to substantiate your self-worth. I know the never-ending need for validation of your outward appearance by men. I know what it's like to give too much of yourself too soon in hopes that it will be reciprocated—and what it's like when it's not. I know the disappointment of only getting a broken heart in return.

Now, without ever having conversations with women, I began to notice how many carried father wounds. I saw these wounds everywhere: in the faces of the young girls I taught as an elementary school teacher, in overwhelmed mothers at the grocery store, in hurting women at church, and in the lives of women I read about in the Bible. One of those biblical women is often overlooked because her story exists in the shadow of her sister's.

The Story of Leah

Leah was the older sister of Rachel who found herself in a complicated polygamous marriage. Her story begins in Genesis 29, when Jacob, the youngest son of Isaac and one of the patriarchs, went to Harran to find a wife from his mother's family. He set out on his journey and providentially arrived at the right well, at the right time, in Paddan Aram.

Prior to Rachel's arrival, Jacob asked the men at the well if they knew Laban, his uncle. As Jacob was talking with them, Rachel was on her way to the well. The men pointed her out in the distance and told Jacob she was Laban's daughter.

Jacob wasted no time. *"He went over and rolled the stone away from the mouth of the well and watered his uncle's sheep. Then Jacob kissed Rachel and began to weep aloud"* (vv. 10–11).

As far as Jacob was concerned, his search for a wife was over. Rachel was the one for him. This would've been a great happily-ever-after ending, but then things got a little complicated.

Once Rachel realized Jacob was her relative, she took him to meet her father, Laban, who hurried to meet Jacob and brought him to his home. He even gave Jacob some affirmation by saying, *"You are my own flesh and blood."* Things were looking promising.

Jacob stayed with Laban for one month before he asked for Rachel's hand in marriage, probably spending as much time with Rachel as he could. His affection for her was likely obvious. Finally, Laban asked Jacob what his wages should be.

His response was indicative of his love for Rachel: *"I'll work for you seven years in return for your younger daughter Rachel"*

(v. 18). Scripture says those seven years *"seemed like only a few days to him because of his love for her"* (v. 20).

Once Jacob served his time, he boldly said to Laban, *"Give me my wife. My time is completed, and I want to make love to her"* (v. 21). He had abstained for seven years and one month, and now he was ready to make Rachel his wife. That night, however, after the wedding feast, Laban took his daughter Leah and gave her to Jacob instead. He made love to the wrong woman.

When Jacob woke up the next morning and discovered he had been given Leah instead of Rachel, he was enraged. What a painful experience this must've been for Leah. She had just consummated the marriage with her future husband only to have him express his disappointment in getting her instead of her sister. She must have felt humiliated, unloved, and devastated. This massive rejection was on top of the fact Leah had grown up overshadowed by her sister's beauty. Scripture describes Leah as having *"weak eyes"* and Rachel as having *"a lovely figure"* and being *"beautiful"* (v. 17).

It does appear that Leah played a role in the fiasco. She had to put on the bridal clothing and disguise herself as her sister, but I'm struck by the words in verse 23: *"He took his daughter Leah and brought her to Jacob, to deceive Jacob."* The verbs *took* and *brought* highlight Laban's intentional actions. He used his own daughter in a scheme to deceive Jacob. She was just a pawn in her father's plan.

Laban should've protected her and had her best interest in mind, but he took advantage of her instead. Surely he knew how much Jacob loved Rachel. Surely he knew Leah's weak eyes had been compared to Rachel's beautiful features all her life. Surely he knew the pain she would endure in this marriage, and yet Laban put Jacob's free labor above his daughter's well-being. As a result, Leah suffered in her union for years.

After Leah's bridal week ended, Scripture says, *"Jacob made love to Rachel also, and his love for Rachel was greater than his love for Leah. And he worked for Laban another seven years"* (v. 30). The Bible doesn't say this, but I believe in addition to Leah's jealousy of her sister, she also had a wound from her father.

She may have questioned how he could place her in that situation. She may have wondered why he didn't tell Jacob he had to wait until Leah was married. She may have been ashamed by the fact that her father resorted to tricking Jacob into marrying her—communicating his doubt that she would ever get married on her own.

When I read Leah's story in the Bible, her father-wounded state stood out to me. She was placed in a difficult situation at the hands of her father, and as a result she had to determine how to continue to live despite what had been done to her. Like Leah, every father-wounded woman must figure this out.

> The good news is, for every woman who's ever contemplated what it would be like to have a different father, whether real or imagined, there's an exchange that is possible.

Our symptoms may vary, but they stem from a relentless root cause that latched itself onto our psyche at some point during our matriculation to adulthood. Unsuspectingly, we opened our hearts to the man we wanted to always protect, always love, and always cherish us. Instead of receiving the former, whether knowingly or unknowingly he took our heart, which we so willingly offered, and wounded us. Though we may attempt to tuck that wound deep within the untouched crannies of our soul, we always know it's there.

This may be why you picked up this book. Maybe you wanted to get some help in processing undealt-with emotions. Maybe you, like me, have perused the aisles in bookstores scanning the list of titles in search of one that fits your ache like a good pair of jeans.

The good news is, for every woman who's ever contemplated what it would be like to have a different father, whether real or imagined, there's an exchange that is possible. Not in the sense where you exchange your father for a better model who possesses all the qualities your father doesn't have. The type of swap I'm referring to is an uneven exchange of father wounds for the extravagant love of God the Father. I stumbled upon it without knowing it was a swap I needed to make.

The Uneven Exchange

My uneven exchange was initiated by five unexpected words from a previous counselor. "Have you forgiven your father?" she asked to my surprise. At the time, I hadn't, nor did I think I needed to (even though I did). Her words were the catalyst to a long and difficult journey to swap my pain for God's love. Several years ago I resolved to do this. It was a path that was oftentimes lonely, seemingly impossible, and one I wanted to quit on many occasions.

On this journey, what I longed for most was a nice, tall, refreshing glass of empathy—someone who understood and could just sit in silence, offer an encouraging word, or provide me with a hug or two without instructions. That's so simple yet so hard to come by. You can't find a prepackaged bottle of empathy at a neighborhood grocery store or anywhere else for that matter. Many times, I went without it.

For years I never made mention of my wounds; they became my best-kept secret. Masterfully, I presented myself as the high-achieving success story. People often saw me as a go-getter, but that was only camouflage in a world that applauds productivity. If anyone ever looked beneath the facade, they would've discovered that I'd become a pro at looking confident when I was scared, happy when I was sad, and beautiful when I didn't think I measured up.

Living like this enables you to talk yourself out of needing to talk about it at all—deceiving yourself into thinking, *I don't have a problem.* You dismiss the sadness that periodically appears when you see a father lovingly interact with his daughter at Target. You ignore the twinge of jealousy when a friend talks about her daddy. You reject the painful memories of your father-daughter relationship, all in an attempt to project an "I'm okay" persona.

It's easier to keep your wounds hidden out of public view. This way you can convince yourself a conversation about your pain is irrelevant and unnecessary. Deep down, you know it's not.

Undealt-with pain will never just go away. It lingers. We can try—unsuccessfully—to suppress it, but eventually it'll resurface. Maybe you've already discovered this.

I want you to know, I'm sorry. I'm sorry that you didn't have the upbringing you wanted. I'm sorry for all the ways you've suffered.

For every time you've ever felt rejected, forgotten, or unloved by your father, I'm sorry. For every event he missed, and your every unnoticed reach for his affection, I'm sorry. If your father was so busy with work that he never made time for you, I'm sorry. If you experienced any form of abuse at the hands of your dad, know that I weep with you. I mourn for the innocence lost, fear injected, and wounds left unhealed.

Where you have experienced far more pain than any woman should ever have to, I'm sorry. If the painful fracture caused by divorce, the stinging loss of abandonment, or the devastating effects of drug and alcohol addiction have left you in despair, know that I'm agonizing over it with you.

Maybe your father left your mother for another woman. Maybe his private life caught up with him and the consequence was incarceration. Maybe he died a premature death and left you longing for a dad who will never come back.

Whatever your situation is, I'm grieving with you. Know that my heart for you reflects the compassion God offers His beloved daughters. He cares about every tear you've ever cried concerning your father, and He grieves with you. As it says in 1 Peter 5:7, *"Cast all your anxiety on him because he cares for you."* He knows the pain you suffered in this relationship is not your fault but rather a by-product of the sin in our world. There's no way you could've caused or prevented your father wounds.

God knows the depths of your pain, and yet He urges you to move toward it in order to be healed. He knows that though what happened to you is extremely painful, it's not the end. Nestled deep within your ache lies resilient hope.

It is this hope that gets you up in the morning. It is this hope that keeps you loving, living, breathing, and believing that the next day will be better than the day before. This is the hope I'm offering you in this book.

It is not a hope of perfect scenarios and happily-ever-after endings. I'm talking about a hope that stares disappointment in the face and chooses not to be defined by it. The hope I'm referring to is a fighter, defiantly defeating every obstacle it faces. This hope is not debilitated by circumstances but overcomes in spite of them.

This is the hope that I pray you discover as you journey through this book. Before we begin, I think it's fitting to acknowledge your pain and give you the necessary time to grieve. Don't keep reading for the sake of putting another coveted check on your "to-do list."

So often we feel an unceasing pressure to keep going despite the loud and deafening internal sirens signaling a problem exists. We keep going, though we need to stop. Today, if that's you, I give you permission to pause. Your healing demands it.

Whether grief hits you two pages over, halfway in, or somewhere near the end of this book, resist the urge to dismiss it. Ignore your phone, turn off the TV, and eliminate every distraction so you can take the necessary time to mourn what's been lost. If you've been holding your emotions hostage because you felt you had to keep it all together, know that you don't have to any longer.

It's time to acknowledge the grief and let it go. I know it's tough. I've walked this tightrope too, teetering somewhere between sorrow and anger, all the while hoping I didn't spiral down to the bottom. But guess what? I've walked through tremendous grief and come out on the other side. This means you can too.

May this book be like your best girlfriend sitting with you in silence and letting you cry as much and for as long as you need to. Grab a box of Kleenex, get a little chocolate, and grieve, sis. You'll thank yourself for it later. I'm giving you this permission because where we're going, grief can't survive. We're leaving the land of "what if" and "if only" and making peace with the beautiful imperfect.

Practical Ways to Begin the Grieving Process

- Express your feelings about your father in a journal.
- Discuss your emotions with a trusted friend.

- Answer the questions for reflection at the end of each chapter. Whether you reflect on them within a group, with a friend, or on your own, take the time to consider your answers and write them down.
- Pray to God about your pain.
- Read and memorize Scripture. You'll find verses that have been helpful to me in the questions for reflection at the end of each chapter.

Questions for Reflection

1. Describe your father. What was he like as a dad?

2. Describe your father-daughter relationship.

3. Have you ever wanted to swap your father out for someone else? Why or why not?

4. How has your father-daughter relationship impacted you and your life?

DIAGNOSING THE OBVIOUS

I was married for eight years before I gave them a name. Haphazardly, I stumbled upon the description one Sunday morning as I sat listening to a message for singles. "Nobody's looking for a woman with daddy wounds," the minister said sarcastically.

Driving the point home, he imitated the pickup line a man might use if he were looking for a father-wounded woman: "You got daddy wounds?" Then, "Ah, I'm not interested in you," he said in response to the imaginary woman's "no" reply. "I want someone who comes into this relationship roaring angry and blames me for everything she's mad at her dad about. That's what I'm looking for."

His fictitious banter impacted me in a way no words had ever done before. *Is that how women with father wounds are perceived?* I thought. I hadn't entertained the idea that a man could tell if a woman had father wounds. Did they talk about this with other men? "Yeah, she's cute, but she's got father wounds," one might say. "Take it from me, you don't want to deal with that." Could men see a woman's wounded state even when she didn't see it for herself? Did they notice it in her body language? Speech? Actions? Choice of clothing? *Why hasn't anyone ever told me this?* I wondered. *Why am I a grown woman just now finding out?*

These thoughts lingered in my mind like flies swarming the baked beans at a family picnic. I considered my questions and thought deeply about myself and my wounds. *He's talking about me,* I reasoned. It was as if someone reached into the darkness and turned on the lights. Immediately, I understood the point the minister was making, as well as how it had been actualized in my own life.

I flashed back to adolescence and every interaction I ever had with the opposite sex. I realized each encounter had, in fact, been influenced by my faulty father-wounded judgment. My poor choices with boys early on in life had been laced with a longing for my father. Every decision had been impacted by the absence of my dad.

Unfortunately, this revelation was about twenty years too late. The time to hear a message like this is before you begin to navigate the dangerous trappings of relationships. A woman needs a father to coach her as she delves into interactions with boys and men. If she doesn't have one, she'll be forced to figure things out on her own. I did (which was problematic). It would've been better had I heard these words prior to venturing into the wide world of men. Consequently, I naively began this rite of passage without knowing anything about father wounds.

That Sunday morning was the first time I'd ever heard this new term, although I was already familiar with its damaging impact. No one in my family had shared this little bit of information. There were no late-night talks about it in my all-women's college. It somehow never came up in my lengthy premarital counseling.

As a result, my wounds were like stowaways on my marital journey. Eventually, they made their presence known in the midst of what should have been a time for my husband and me to discover each other and build a future together. Whether it was during simple conversations, sex, or arguments, these wounds made frequent cameos, letting me know they were present. I couldn't explain or define them. I hadn't taken the time to determine the root cause of my issues.

> **A woman needs a father to coach her as she delves into interactions with boys and men. If she doesn't have one, she'll be forced to figure things out on her own.**

All of these thoughts overwhelmed me as I sat in my seat reflecting on the message that Sunday morning. It felt like I was being forced to deal with my raw and unhealed places. The pastor's words intermingled with the part of me that was already painfully aware that I had a problem.

After the service ended, I just sat in the balcony feeling all exposed and helpless. It was as if my brokenness had been shared on social media and then went viral. Making a beeline for my soul, the words *daddy wounds* zeroed in on an ache I had been sensing for more than a decade.

I first noticed this ache in my teenage years. I had this insatiable need for attention, and not just from males (although that was a factor). I was like a bottomless pit longing for affirmation from any source.

Nothing was ever enough.

Combined with my people-pleasing addiction, insecurity began to grow and thrive. As a result, I felt the need to outperform, out-compete, and outdo everyone in order to maintain my sense of self.

Performance became my crutch, anesthetizing the reality that I didn't deem myself lovable. I subconsciously purposed to prove I was deserving of love by working for it. I was caught in what professional counselor Robert S. McGee calls "the performance trap" in his book *The Search for Significance*, addicted to the perpetual cycle of achievement and validation.[1]

Though I am naturally motivated to excel, there's a difference between working because you're driven to and working because you're afraid not to. Fear of losing value in the eyes of people should never be the motivating factor for our accomplishments.

But I feared everything.

Failure, people's opinions, and the successes of other women were all threats to my self-worth. What I feared most was not being important. So I fought to maintain titles, status, and ac-colades, clinging to what I believed was my identity.

This was a futile attempt. Eventually, when the performance stopped, so did the affirmation, and I was left alone with my thoughts and low self-esteem. Which is why I felt so outed that cold Sunday morning in February—and that was just one of the many feelings I had circulating internally. I also wanted to throw myself one big ol' pity party right there in the sanctuary.

Part of me had a strong desire to take a sledgehammer to a piece of drywall, releasing anger and pent-up frustration with every blow.

It isn't fair.
I didn't ask for this.
I deserve better.

A ton of emotions bombarded me. Sadness, anger, fear, discouragement, frustration, and shame all formed the perfect storm and took turns tormenting me. I was a mess—correction, a hot mess. My new revelation only exasperated and exposed the chaos that had been going on inside of me.

Although I was relieved to hear my dysfunction named, I was also completely jacked up—overwhelmed by the size of the problem, sad that I had a problem to begin with, and frustrated by the dominant role those pesky wounds were already playing in my life.

I was left with my diagnosis, my daddy wounds, and all my emotions (which is not a safe place to be). What I needed was some advice, wisdom, and HELP immediately.

If there were any support groups of sisters saying, "Girrrrl, me too!" I didn't know about them. As far as I knew, women occasionally talked about their wounds on Father's Day, when it was relevant. Then the conversation died down on Monday, only to resurface the next June when it was relevant again.

> **Fear of losing value in the eyes of people should never be the motivating factor for our accomplishments.**

I couldn't go to my family doctor for these wounds. They weren't like the flu or asthma. This was a sickness of the heart with no known treatment plan. I wasn't aware of medicinal options, traditional or naturopathic.

If there were any, those of us suffering from father wounds would need multiple treatment options to cover the vast and varied degree of our wounds. These options would depend on several factors: when the wound occurred, the size and depth of the wound, the impact, and whether we had been able to heal.

I discovered this as I began to engage with women on the internet. Some women had minor abrasions; they were wounded by occasional and insensitive statements from their fathers. Other women experienced painful incisions that healed but left scars as unforgettable mementos. Some women had deeper lacerations. These women carried the weight of difficult circumstances that left them crippled in some way. I encountered women with puncture wounds that penetrated to the core of their soul. Finally, there were women with the most severe type of wounds that left forcible tears to their heart.

Through connecting with women of differing ages, races, and backgrounds, I realized that saying a woman had father wounds was a narrow description; limiting the scope of the problem to two words was insufficient. Although the words *daddy wounds* offered a level of understanding, there was still so much that needed to be defined for me.

That two-word phrase needed to be unpacked. Inner healing demanded I identify the specific types of wounds that impacted me. I began to name them: trust, affirmation, love, acceptance, identity, provision, and significance wounds were a few that I noticed in me. I had a diagnosis and a general understanding of some of my symptoms, but what I longed for was a cure—a lasting solution for my wounded state. After all, I had been this way long before my Sunday morning diagnosis.

Now I had a decision to make. On the one hand, I could choose to dismiss my diagnosis like it didn't apply to me. I could continue to mask it with achievement, cover it with my appearance, or crowd it out with people and events. On the other hand, I could deal with it by choosing the less-traveled path of healing and wholeness.

The Woman with an Issue of Blood

The Bible tells us of another woman who had to make a choice to move in the direction of healing. In Matthew 9, Mark 5, and Luke 8, we learn of a woman who had been subject to bleeding for twelve years. She is introduced to us not by her name but by her physical condition. Her medical state became her identity. No longer was she seen as a human being with thoughts, emotions, and a need to be loved. She was now known as a woman with an issue of blood.

We don't know her background or family makeup, but we can speculate what her life must have been like. This woman was possibly ostracized, judged, and criticized. Nosy neighbors may have questioned why she had a discharge. They may have assumed it was because she sinned. Town gossips likely talked about her behind her back. This woman was isolated from others, and as a result she may have experienced loneliness, fear, shame, and depression. She was desperate for a change.

Hemorrhaging women, and anyone or anything they touched, were considered unclean. To be deemed clean, she had to first overcome the insurmountable odds of being healed. Once that took place, she would have to wait seven days and then take two doves and two pigeons to the priest so he could atone for her uncleanness. Today, we'd call that a lot of red tape standing between her and her healing.

Year after year she continued to believe healing was within reach, even though she repeatedly experienced setbacks. Scripture tells us that this woman *"suffered a great deal under the care of many doctors and had spent all she had, yet instead of getting better she grew worse"* (Mark 5:26). In addition to her chronic illness, she was broke. This woman had every reason to curl up into the fetal position and completely give up hope, but she didn't.

In what seems to be a leap of faith, she made the decision to go and see Jesus. *"She said to herself, 'If I only touch his cloak, I will be healed'"* (Matt. 9:21). This woman simply heard about Jesus. She hadn't experienced a miracle up close and personal. She'd never met Him face-to-face. But none of that mattered because she was desperate for a change and believed Jesus could heal her.

This time the stakes were raised in her pursuit of healing. Her risky idea required coming out from the shadows and into the public. She would have to go to Jesus in the midst of the crowd, running the risk of touching several people along the way. It might have created a scene.

Then there was the possibility that this last attempt might not even work. I imagine doubt and fear chimed in with their two cents, whispering, "This time could be like all the other times. You could not only walk away unhealed, you could also be humiliated in the process." This unnamed woman had a lot to lose, but she deemed her healing as worth the risk.

She had resilient hope and it paid off, because immediately after she touched Jesus's cloak, *"her bleeding stopped, and she felt in her body that she was freed from her suffering"* (Mark

5:29). That moment must have been overwhelming. After twelve long years of continual bleeding, she was instantly healed. At this realization, many people would want to share their good news with the entire world, but this woman preferred slipping inconspicuously into the crowd. She didn't want to be identified or noticed because it was forbidden for her to be there. But Jesus would not allow her to remain in obscurity. *"'Who touched me?' Jesus asked"* (Luke 8:45).

Here we see the omniscient Savior asking, *"Who touched me?"* I believe it wasn't because He was unsure whose hands grasped the edge of His outer garment. Jesus knew the exact moment the woman's fingers touched His tunic and caused miraculous power to leave His body. This was God made flesh: creator, sustainer, ruler, all-powerful, present everywhere, and all-knowing. He had to have known who touched Him. I believe Jesus asked the question not for His own benefit but for the woman's. He knew she had spent more than a decade in the shadows of society and needed to be publicly declared healed and clean before everyone. He also knew she needed to be affirmed, and so He persisted: *"Someone touched me; I know that power has gone out from me"* (v. 46).

He left the unnamed woman no choice. She had to make her presence known. I imagine she reluctantly rose from a low position. Tears slowly trickled down her face, and she trembled with fear and moved to the forefront. Then in an act of worship and gratitude, she fell at the feet of Jesus. The text tells us that she then told Him the whole truth.

Jesus could have chastised this woman for touching Him. He could have publicly condemned her action, but He opted instead to patiently listen to her. Right there in front of a massive and potentially judgmental crowd, He was all ears. How comforting this must have been! Then, *"He said to her, 'Daughter, your faith has healed you. Go in peace and be freed from your suffering'"* (Mark 5:34).

This is where we see a loving and compassionate God redefining this unnamed woman. If there was any doubt in anyone's mind regarding this woman and her healing, Jesus cleared it up once and for all. He not only declared her healed, He called her "daughter." He did not say "unnamed woman" or "woman with an issue of blood." He selected the intimate and tender term *daughter*. With that one word He said, "You are not alone."

"You are not isolated."
"You are My beloved daughter."
"Be freed from your suffering."

Jesus came alongside this woman in the midst of the crowd and He validated her. Now she didn't have to be known as that woman with an issue of blood. She could be known as the woman Jesus healed. She could be known as a beloved daughter of God.

I identified with this woman.
I too had an issue.
I too had suffered for many years.
I too had an option to either remain
unchanged or pursue my healing.

Seeking Our Own Healing

Maybe you can relate. Maybe you find yourself at an impasse—deciding whether it's worth it to unearth repressed pain as it relates to your father. Maybe choosing healing and wholeness feels too risky. I understand, and I found myself at this very juncture right before I reasoned the reward was far greater than the risk. The promise of exchanging my wounds for God's extravagant love was one I could not pass up.

The pursuit of healing and wholeness is an option for every woman with a father wound. Pursuit indicates we must take action. For the unnamed woman, her pursuit involved making her way through the crowd to touch the hem of Jesus's outer garment. It was difficult, risky, and necessary. Sis, our healing is not going to fall from the sky. There are actions we must take.

Choosing this path is not easy, and it will most likely cost us something. It will require vulnerability. We'll have to relinquish our pride and admit that we've been impacted by our father wounds. We may even have to acknowledge the fact that we need help.

> **Sis, our healing is not going to fall from the sky. There are actions we must take.**

The road to wholeness is tailor-made for each individual, full of unique challenges we must overcome. There are, however, pivotal steps to healing that each of us must take. The first of those steps is acknowledging we have a father wound. Our healing journey can't begin until we make this critical declaration.

Acknowledging our wounds appears simple, but it can be quite difficult. It requires admitting we have a problem. We have to be honest about how our father's actions impacted us. This means we revisit the times when we experienced rejection, shame, abandonment, and hurt at the hand of our father, whether it was done knowingly or unknowingly, and we allow ourselves to say, "That (word or action) wounded me."

Admittance would be easier if we were talking about the actions of a random stranger, but we're not. We're talking about the actions of our father, and the word *father* comes with a range of emotions. Some of us have fond memories intermingled with wounds when it comes to our father. Others of us are holding onto hope that our father will change. Many of us are attempting to mask the reality of who our father is with the idea of who we want him to be. This is because of an innate desire for closeness with the man who gave us life.

In his book *Bringing Up Girls*, Dr. James Dobson says, "There is a place in the female soul reserved for Daddy, or a daddy figure, that will yearn for affirmation. Not every girl or woman is the same, of course, but almost every girl desires a close bond with this most significant man in her life. She will adore him if he loves and protects her and if she finds safety and warmth in his arms. She will feel that way throughout life unless he disappoints her or until one of them dies."[2]

By design, we're wired to love our fathers, and as a result things can get complicated when we are tasked with admitting we have father wounds. In the name of love and happiness, we're tempted to cover a multitude of wrongs on his part. For the sake of keeping the family gatherings upbeat, we would rather not say anything and just let bygones be bygones.

We don't want to be the family member who ruins the get-together, so we either remain silent, withdraw, become a different version of ourselves, or avoid the gathering altogether. For many of us, we wrestle with the reality that acknowledging our wounds may depict our father in a negative light. It may place a blemish on his reputation and diminish who he is in the eyes of others.

For this reason we may opt to protect our fathers and conceal our pain—sometimes for years, sometimes forever. I get it and I've done it, but this won't help us overcome our father wounds. What it will do is keep the door to our healing and wholeness padlocked.

I understand the temptation to ignore, dismiss, deny, and pretend when it comes to our father wounds. I want to encourage you to glean from the courage of the unnamed woman and pursue healing no matter what it costs you. Remember how she made her way through a crowd that had no understanding of all the days and ways she had suffered? Think about her resolve to reach out to Jesus, and press your way through every obstacle that stands between you and your healing.

In saying that, I'm not asking you to grab a megaphone and make a public declaration at the Thanksgiving dinner table either. What I'm suggesting is a private time of self-reflection. Give yourself permission to admit you have father wounds. Allow yourself the time and space to acknowledge how your father's actions, whether intentional or not, wounded you. This initial step unlocks the door to our healing. It is here our pursuit of wholeness begins. Although the journey is scary and unfamiliar, we don't have to be hesitant to pursue healing. Just as God affirmed the unnamed woman for her faith and willingness to pursue healing, He does the same for us.

You, like me, may find yourself frustrated by your wounds and grieved by the impact they've had in your life. Although I was in this place, I chose to take my diagnosis and pursue healing and wholeness, just like the unnamed woman. You can do it too. Take the first step in pursuit of your healing and know the reward far outweighs the risk.

Practical Ways to Process Your Father Wounds

- Express your feelings about your father in a journal.
- Discuss your emotions with a trusted friend.
- Answer the questions for reflection at the end of each chapter.
- Pray to God about your pain.
- Read and memorize Scripture.

Questions for Reflection

1. Read and memorize 1 Peter 5:7.
2. When did you first hear the term *father wound/daddy wound*?
3. What does this term mean to you?
4. Do you believe women with father wounds have observable characteristics?
5. As you unpack your father wounds, what type of wounds do you discover (i.e., trust, affirmation, acceptance, love, identity, provision, and significance)?
6. How do you think father wounds have impacted you? Your thoughts? Actions? Beliefs?
7. What painful experiences did you have with your father?
8. What types of things have you done to heal from your father wounds?

3

INTERROGATING THE PAST

God seems to speak to me on road trips. Whether I'm staring down an unending highway on the driver's side or sitting in the passenger seat attempting to read between periodic nods and incessant mind drifts, God speaks. It was on one of these road trips that He initiated a journey of another kind.

I was trying to read a new book when an unexpected exploratory trek into my heart and mind began. My reading goal was ambitious, but with a six-hour drive back to Atlanta from Virginia, I figured I would be able to get at least midway through my new read by the time we arrived home. I had high hopes of devouring this book quickly and accumulating more information to help me on my quest to resolve my daddy wound dilemma. On a mission, I would not stop until I'd compiled all my research into a book for women just like me.

I purposed to write for those who found themselves at an impasse with their wounds and needed a practical guide of just what to do about them. So, I decided to gather information and document my journey along the way. Why not turn all the information I was learning into a resource that other women could benefit from?

What I failed to realize was that I'm a human being and not a robot. Healing from father wounds requires more than research and self-help books. Genuine healing and wholeness need time and the supernatural intervention of God. I naively assumed that a father wound diagnosis combined with a little bit of reading was a license to write a book; it wasn't. Thankfully, God had meticulously crafted an intervention for me.

I'd selected *Bringing Up Girls: Practical Advice and Encouragement for Those Shaping the Next Generation of Women* as my road trip read. This book, by Dr. James Dobson, takes a comprehensive look at the development of a woman from birth to adulthood. It's a little over 250 pages, and as we progressed down I-85, I was planning to knock out several of them—until I got to chapter 2, "Girls in Peril."

As I read, I found myself unable to continue reading. Research slowly evolved into an unwanted therapy session as the book began to take aim at my broken heart. Dobson described girls today and how some pursued guys in an effort to experience the affirmation they craved. Words and phrases like *longing for love, pleasure, adolescent,* and *relationships* flashed on the page at me like lights in the darkness. He culminated the paragraph by saying the behavior of the girls was linked to something they were missing from their fathers.

I was missing something from my father.

Honestly, I didn't even make it through the paragraph. I found it increasingly difficult to emotionally disconnect from the words I was reading. They were no longer about unknown females; they were about me. This was the life I had lived in an attempt to secure the love and validation I so desperately needed growing up. In that moment I evolved from being the researcher seeking information, into the human subject being observed. I was the girl he was referring to who had naively exhibited these behaviors. I was the one who physically and emotionally opened myself up to the opposite sex looking for the affection I craved from my daddy.

And as I sat on the passenger side of the car with my lofty reading goals, I instantly knew that I wasn't going to get past chapter 2. I closed the tearstained book, covered my face with my hands, bent over, and sobbed—and not a little sniffle either.

This was an all-out ugly cry that unexpectedly held me hostage. My tears reached back and grabbed unaddressed childhood pain. I felt hopeless, and I couldn't stop crying or explain why I was crying to my husband, who sat in the driver's seat watching the whole thing transpire. I was grieving years of suppressed emotions that had suddenly come to the surface.

As I read those words from chapter 2, my mind went back to my initial interaction with boys. It wasn't pretty. In fact, it really wasn't anything I wanted to remember or think about. But this was the place I found myself. The dam had been breached, and years of shame, guilt, and regret flowed through freely. I was beginning to understand that healing myself and creating a pathway for others to follow wasn't going to be as easy as I originally thought.

It wasn't as simple as gathering facts and filling the pages of a book. Writing about the subject of father wounds required that I get healed and whole first, and grieving the impact of my father wounds while riding down I-85 was just the beginning. During that road trip I realized God was not going to allow me to write about something I hadn't walked through. In His sovereignty, He drilled this fact home by initiating multiple experiences for me to process the impact of my father wounds.

Secret(ive) Admirers

Mr. Gomez was my seventh-grade teacher. He was a tall man with a thick accent, black-rimmed glasses, and thinning, curly brown hair. He was what I've termed the logical-mathematical type: clad in khaki cotton Dockers and a plaid shirt every day. He was a kind and gentle man who probably would have made an excellent teacher somewhere else, but he couldn't control our mischievous class of tweens to save his life. It was a difficult year, and I'm not sure who was more traumatized—him or me.

I attended a small private school on the south side of Fort Worth, Texas. I'd previously attended a larger and more culturally diverse Catholic school that left me with fond memories of class parties, Ash Wednesday, and fall carnivals. That school offered more resources, better facilities, lots of friends, and absolutely no bullies, which I couldn't say about my new school.

From my first day at the new school until the day I left three years later, I was teased constantly. Everything about me was fair game: the way I talked, my nonexistent breasts, my skinny legs, and my broad nose that made me the brunt of classroom jokes by males and females alike. For a burgeoning insecure preteen in a single-parent household, this laid the foundation for the perfect storm in my adolescence.

As tumultuous as the first year was, I do have fond memories of Mr. Gomez reading through *James and the Giant Peach* by

Roald Dahl. Somehow when he read this children's narrative about James discovering the magical world of an overgrown peach filled with large talking insects, life didn't seem so bad. When he was reading I would escape, even if only for a moment, the intense and constant bullying I experienced from my classmates.

When Mr. Gomez read from the pages of this book, I would easily get lost in the pictures his words painted in my mind. Here there were no jabs, name-calling, or highly inappropriate gestures; it was just Mr. Gomez's words and my imagination freeing me from my seventh-grade prison.

There was, however, another person worth mentioning: a boy we'll call David, who secretly took an interest in me. I'm not sure when or how he asked me for my number, but I gladly fulfilled his request with excitement. Someone actually wanted to talk to me. Of all the girls in my class, he thought I was cute—the awkward, flat-chested girl with a big nose and merciless acne. Me, the girl whose self-esteem was so dangerously low that I would have fallen for any guy who expressed an interest in me. And I did.

My secret admirer was no admirer at all. He was just a secret. The only time he acknowledged his feelings for me was on the phone, late at night and in private. Not once did he ever speak up when I needed him to. Never did he ever say, "She's with me," or simply, "Stop picking on her." On the contrary, he didn't want anyone to know that he was talking to me at all.

I not only tolerated his secret interest in me, I welcomed it with delight. He thought I was cute—girlfriend worthy. A flesh-and-blood boy had wanted my number and actually called me on the phone.

It was exciting for me to be liked, desired, and wanted. I loved the feeling it initiated in me, and I wanted to experience it over and over again. In some regards, that feeling became like a drug and I was an addict; I did what I had to do to maintain my high.

When David called, I answered. I was willing to accept his sub-par treatment because, in my opinion, it was better than no treatment at all. Sometimes we tolerate unacceptable behavior from others because we don't know we deserve better. But we are worth more and we don't have to settle.

I needed someone to look into my young impressionable eyes and tell me I was beautiful. I needed to know my worth had absolutely nothing to do with my anatomy and everything to do with who God made me to be. I desperately needed the affirmation of my father.

John and Stasi Eldredge describe this need in their book *Captivating: Unveiling the Mystery of a Woman's Soul*. They wrote:

> Little girls want to know, Am I lovely? The twirling skirts, the dress up, the longing to be pretty and to be seen—that is what that's all about. We are seeking an answer to our Question. When I was a girl of maybe five years old, I remember standing on top of the coffee table in my grandparents' living room and singing my heart out. I wanted to capture attention—especially my father's attention. I wanted to be captivating. We all did. But for most of us, the answer to our Question when we were young was "No, there is nothing captivating about you." Get off the coffee table. Nearly all a woman does in her adult life is fueled by her longing to be delighted in, her longing to be beautiful, to be irreplaceable, to have her Question answered, "Yes!" . . .
>
> And down in the depths of our hearts, our Question remains. Unanswered. Or rather, it remains answered in the way it was answered so badly in our youth. "Am I lovely? Do you see me? Do you want to see me? Are you captivated by what you find in me?" We live haunted by that question, yet unaware that it still needs an answer.[1]

I needed my daddy to lay the foundation for my interaction with the opposite sex. He should have been the first man to ever tell me I was beautiful, wanted, or valuable. His affection should have been the first I experienced from the male gender. He should have been the one to educate me on what I should and shouldn't expect from a man. I needed my dad to see the emptiness in me and how he held the power to fill it. Those needs, however, were something my father could not meet.

> **Sometimes we tolerate unacceptable behavior from others because we don't know we deserve better.**

This early experience with David became my modus operandi for interacting with the male gender. After David, there was a string of other boys. Each of those relationships involved increasing secrecy, physical contact, shame, regret, and guilt. Most were characterized by lust and left me feeling dirty and ashamed yet unable to break free from the addictive and debilitating cycle.

Inwardly, I believed I was confident and beautiful. I saw myself as a leader with great ideas and a vibrant personality. This belief, however, wasn't enough to satisfy me. I knew who I longed to be, but I also wrestled with an insatiable need to be liked, loved, and desired by males. As a result, my behavior was self-sabotaging: moving from one person to the next, afraid to be alone as if this state was an admission to the world that I was unworthy of love.

So I stayed coupled up: always in a relationship, whether public or secret. This provided the security I lacked. I clung to this un-healthy security blanket of sorts, allowing it to comfort me from seventh grade to adulthood. I feared that if I didn't perform, the relationship would end and I would be alone again. Left on my own, I would have to face feelings of not measuring up: never being pretty, smart, or worthy enough to be loved for who I was as a person rather than what someone could get from me in return. I accepted the lie that to keep a guy's attention and maintain my sense of self, I needed to perform.

Perfect performance became my antidote for abandonment. I did my best to walk the tightrope of precision: dotting i's and crossing t's. Consequently, every time I smiled—though I was hurting, kept silent when I wanted to speak, or lied to keep the peace—I was subliminally saying, "Stay!" to the person I was in a relationship with.

Don't go, walk away, or leave the room.
Resist the urge to hang up the phone.
Choose to lean in when you want to run.
Speak when you'd rather be quiet.
Make eye contact when you want to look the other way.

At the root of all these statements was the same desperate plea: *Don't abandon me!*

If actions hinted at the possibility of someone leaving me, it triggered the ache I had for my father's affection. The end of a relationship set off an internal panic in me. I felt lost without a relationship.

I never uttered the words "I am unwanted," but my actions demonstrated how this lie was driving my behavior. This unspoken false belief revealed the blinding influence my father wounds played in my life as a girl and a woman. The damage inflicted was not a onetime occurrence but was hauntingly revisited in every relationship with the opposite sex. I was left with the lingering question whether the next male would leave me just like my father did.

Relationships, however, are not designed to secure and sustain a woman. We don't have to live in fear, second-guessing the commitment of the men in our lives. Nor do we have to perform to keep them. We

> **Relationships are not designed to secure and sustain a woman.**

are free to be the woman God has created us to be, resting in the fact that we are already loved, wanted, and completely accepted by our Father in heaven. His love never changes. Unfortunately, I didn't learn this lesson in my adolescent years.

Searching for Unconditional Love

I grew up in the talk show era. Sally Jesse Raphael, Geraldo, Dona-hue, Montel, Jerry Springer, and Oprah dominated the airwaves. In the 1980s it seemed every other interview featured teenage girls who wanted to have a baby. When asked about their motivation for wanting a child, on more than one occasion the reply was, "I just want somebody to love and to love me back."

In hindsight I've found myself questioning why no one ever asked about the father of these girls. No one seemed to delve deep enough into the issue in order to identify the root cause of their behavior. Why did they not feel loved? What was lacking in their life that would cause them to think an infant could provide the unconditional love they longed for?

I might not have wanted a baby, but in desperation I too searched for unconditional love. The same needs these girls grappled with on national television I wrestled with in the privacy of my own thoughts. I knew the ache to be loved, touched, held, affirmed, cherished, encouraged, and valued. Although I didn't cross the threshold of virginity prior to marriage, I made several bad decisions regarding male relationships that stemmed (in part) from a longing I had for the love and affirmation of my biological father. I believe these young girls had the same unmet need, but at that time there was no connection made between their desire for a baby and father wounds.

According to the National Fatherhood Initiative, teens without fathers are twice as likely to be involved in early sexual activity and seven times more likely to get pregnant in adolescence. The National Center for Fathering has cited a study with a sampling of 1,409 rural adolescents that indicated "adolescents in father-absence homes were more likely to report being sexually active compared to adolescents living with their fathers."[2] Thus, there is a connection between the relationship a girl has with her father and her subsequent interactions with the male gender. It may seem that a woman's sexual decisions are in no way related to the relationship she has with her father, but the data above suggests otherwise.

Author H. Norman Wright offers additional insight in his book *Always Daddy's Girl: Understanding Your Father's Impact on Who You Are*. In it he says,

> It is from her father that a girl needs to know that she is attractive, that her conversation is interesting and that her creativity is worthwhile. If her father applauds her mental and spiritual attributes during her formative years, she will learn not to rely solely on shallow qualities like sex appeal to attract men as an adult. Affirmation from her father in proper doses will convince her that she is an important person, not a sex object.[3]

The role of the father is critical in laying the foundation for how girls and women will interact with the opposite sex. In an oversexed culture that says, "Have as much sex as you want, with whomever you want, whenever you want," this pivotal information from H. Norman Wright seems to be missing. Collectively we need to take a closer look at the physiological causes and ramifications for early sexual activity and promiscuous behavior.

If a father-wounded daughter learns to perform sexually in order to receive affirmation and validation in return, it creates a stimulus response that is difficult to break. In fact, when a woman has sex with a man, the hypothalamus area of her brain is activated, releasing the hormone oxytocin into the bloodstream. Known as "the love hormone," it promotes bonding and binds women emotionally to their partner. As a result, women with multiple sexual partners will begin to release less oxytocin with each physical encounter. The potential result over time is an inability to attach and connect to one man sexually for the rest of her life.[4]

If this is how a woman comes to know love, she will continue to engage in various forms of sexual behavior to get the love she desperately longs for. She will compromise everything to get it, including but not limited to her values, her sense of self, her desires, and what she ultimately wants in a relationship with a man. In search of the love she didn't receive as a child, she may consciously or unconsciously go from man to man and bed to bed, equating love with sex or sexual acts.

One glance, touch, or word from the opposite sex is enough to create a flurry of activity in our bodies. Signals race, temperatures rise, hormones are released, and we're led like sheep to the slaughter by our emotions. Although God gave us feelings, our feelings don't always represent truth.

In fact, emotions can deceive us with convincing rationale. "This feels right!" "He's the one." "I deserve to be happy!" "This one is different." And so boy meets girl, and the two experience what appears to be chemistry. The conversation is great. You can talk for hours. He makes you laugh, and you have so much in common. The natural progression seems like it should be a sexual relationship.

Then passion and ecstasy replace common sense, and for a moment, emotional deception clouds sound judgment. But when the cloud lifts and the light of clarity shines through, we are left with the result of our deceit: disappointment, regret, shame, and guilt. I too have borne these unwanted consequences many times over, and we're not alone. According to H. Norman Wright, women who grow up without the love and affirmation of their fathers are susceptible to finding themselves in physical relationships prior to marriage.[5]

Love vs. Its Impostors

Many times I have thought I was in love, but when I measured those relationships against the types of love in the Bible, I realized what drove many of them was not love at all. The Bible mentions four types of love.

Agape love is selfless, sacrificial, and unconditional love. This is the love that moved God the Father to send His Son to earth on behalf of humanity. *Eros* love is the physical, sensual love between a husband and a wife. We see this love in the book of Song of Solomon as we read the dialogue between a young woman and her lover. *Philia* love is close friendship or brotherly love. Jonathan demonstrated this type of love toward David (1 Sam. 18:1–5). *Storge* love is family love, the bond among mothers, fathers, sisters, and brothers. This is the type of love Ruth demonstrated when she opted to go with her mother-in-law, Naomi, to Bethlehem instead of returning to Moab (Ruth 1).

A committed marital relationship should include all four types of love, and a dating relationship should have three of the four. Sex outside of marriage, no matter how great the "chemistry," is not the eros kind of love—thus reducing that mountaintop feeling to lust.

So what would drive a woman to stay with a man if she wasn't truly loved by him? Although the answers are varied and too numerous to narrow down, I'll zero in on one that was the impetus behind my behavior.

The unsettling truth is, at the time, I didn't believe I was worthy of love, so I settled, afraid that I'd lose the substitute if I raised my standard for the real. This is the subtle lie low self-esteem tells you. "If you have boundaries, he will leave. If you refuse to accept this treatment, you'll be alone. It is better to have someone than no one at all."

Love, however, debunks the lies that fear tells us. Love desires to give and not get, wait and not rush, and sacrifice rather than indulge. Love looks, sounds, and feels like God. For His daughters, this is the example He gave and the standard He set for our male-female relationships. His Word is the barometer for our interactions with the opposite sex. Thus, we are enabled to let go of our substitutes and are freed to believe that God is more than capable of providing us with the real thing. God compels every woman to raise her standards for relationships with the opposite sex because we're worth more than a love substitute. The challenge for every father-wounded woman is to recognize that she is deserving of unconditional love.

> **Love looks, sounds, and feels like God.**

The Past Affects the Present

"I'm not going to stop having sex," a friend said confidently. She was a sexually active Christian with a "don't challenge me on this issue" mindset. Her statement was firm and indicated that she would not be willing to change her position on the matter. Our relationship had been birthed in confrontation, so I wasn't taken aback by the declaration she made on our mani-pedi girls' day, and I decided to challenge her.

I wanted her to think about the psychological reasons driving her behavior. I wanted her to entertain the possibility that her sexual appetite might have been driven by an ache she had for the affirmation of her father. I wanted her to reconsider her position. She, however, was not interested in what I wanted.

Needless to say, the conversation didn't end well. In fact, our parting gifts were battle scars from our heated verbal swap. After that day I thought often about the words she said and the ones I didn't. I wish I had said that it's not the act that qualifies me to speak, but the ache—for I know it well. The root cause of our actions was an innate desire to be loved. Both of us had compromised physically to garner the love we craved.

If I'd had a bit more wisdom and a lot more grace, I would've focused on her heart and not her behavior. This is what Jesus did when He walked the face of the earth. He demonstrated unparalleled compassion for humanity; balancing grace and truth, He zeroed in on the heart condition of all humankind, not the behaviors. We see this in His tender interaction with the woman caught in adultery.

In John 8 we're introduced to this unnamed woman. Mired in shame and embarrassment, she was placed between an indignant, self-righteous crowd and a humble and compassionate Savior.

The Pharisees and religious leaders used this woman as a ploy to trap Jesus. They said to Him, *"In the Law Moses commanded us to stone such women. Now what do you say?"* (v. 5).

I imagine they smugly stood back and waited on Jesus's response while the crowd watched in suspense. Then Jesus, being the embodiment of the law, responded in an unexpected way. He bent down and began writing something on the ground with His finger. No one saw this coming.

The woman was most likely full of anxiety as she awaited her fate. Surely the moment was ripe with intensity as Jesus held her future in His hand.

His response demonstrated matchless wisdom, infinite compassion, and unparalleled grace: *"Let any one of you who is without sin be the first to throw a stone at her"* (v. 7). The Scriptures say the crowd immediately began to dissipate. One by one the members of this hostile bunch reasoned it was better to walk away than cast a stone, until only Jesus and the woman remained.

I wish I could've seen the look on her face as she watched all her accusers slowly walk away. Maybe she previously assumed Jesus was going to say, "You're right. She should be stoned." Maybe she watched her life flash before her eyes. I imagine her head was down, because this is typically the posture we take when we feel ashamed. I can see this woman slowly lifting her head as she hears footsteps leave the scene and move farther off into the distance. Eventually, her head stops rising and she meets the eyes of her Savior.

Jesus looked at her not as a sinful woman but as a beloved and cherished daughter of God. He was essentially giving her the tough love she needed to fully understand that she was worth so much more than what she had settled for.

This tender moment displayed the heart of God in grand fashion. When Christ found Himself alone with this woman, He didn't condemn her, nor did He condone her actions. He said, *"Woman, where are they? Has no one condemned you? . . . Then neither do I condemn you. . . . Go now and leave your life of sin"* (vv. 10–11). A holy God looked at a sinful woman and told her not to return to adulterous living.

When considering this woman, I've often wondered about her backstory. How did she end up in an adulterous relationship to begin with? What felt need did this relationship provide for her? Did the unidentified man make her feel loved, wanted, or desired? Had she tried to leave this life before? Where was the man she was caught in adultery with? Where was her father?

> **When we find ourselves mired in our shame and guilt, God draws near to us and loves us lavishly.**

Although John doesn't give us the answers to these questions, what we know for certain is the lure of this relationship was greater than the fear of being punished. Something compelled this woman to engage in a forbidden relationship. And though John doesn't tell us what happened next, I believe she left with a resolve to follow Jesus's command. I believe this woman followed Christ's instruction because she came face-to-face with the unexplainable love and mercy of God. Out of gratitude for His lavish and unconditional love, I believe she changed her behavior once and for all.

You, like me, may see yourself in this unnamed woman. You may be able to identify with the shame of her actions, guilt of her sin, and regret of her choices. If that's the case, know that God's response to you is the same as His response to this woman. For every father-wounded woman who has ever attempted to get her needs met by the opposite sex, our loving and compassionate heavenly Father says, *"Neither do I condemn you. . . . Go now and leave your life of sin."*

God isn't standing over us with a pointed finger. He doesn't blame, accuse, or abandon us. When we find ourselves mired in our shame and guilt, God draws near to us and loves us lavishly. Without a need to explain why or how we find ourselves in this plight, His response to us is the same.

If God doesn't condemn us, we shouldn't condemn ourselves either. As it says in Romans 8:1, *"Therefore, there is now no condemnation for those who are in Christ Jesus."* We must forgive ourselves for the ways we've attempted to meet our needs. This includes sexual sin. God doesn't condemn us, but He does correct us. He delineates the behavior that is sinful and contrary to His words. Essentially, He is telling us, "Daughter, there's a better way." Resist the temptation to meet your needs in the flesh, and trust that our omnipotent God is capable of meeting the needs your biological father did not.

Practical Ways
to Begin Evaluating Your Relationships with Men

- Answer the small group discussion questions.
- Express your feelings in a journal.
- Discuss your emotions with a trusted friend.
- Join a support group.
- Pray to God about your pain.

Questions for Reflection

1. Read and memorize 1 Corinthians 6:18; Galatians 2:20; 1 John 1:9; and 1 John 3:1.

2. What did your father teach you about the opposite sex?

3. What do you believe about your self-worth? (Read Psalm 139 and then complete the rest of this question.) What does God believe about you? Do you have any thoughts about yourself that do not line up with God's thoughts about you?

4. In what ways have you attempted to receive affirmation from males that you did not receive from your father?

5. Have you based your self-worth on your physical anatomy? How might God be leading you to base your identity on who He says you are?

6. If you're single, do you feel the need to be in a relationship in order to be secure? How might God be leading you to derive your sense of security from Him?

7. If you're currently in a sexual relationship outside of marriage, how might God be leading you in a different direction?

WRESTLING WITH
THE REAL

My husband proposed six months after we started dating. I was fresh out of college and secretly hoping I would meet my forever knight when he walked up to me one Sunday evening after church. "Hi, Kia," he said as if he had rehearsed those words a thousand times. "I was interested in getting to know you a little better and wanted to see if you would consider going out on a date with me?" As he stood there waiting for my response, I was already thinking, *He's the one*.

I guess you could say I was jumping the gun a bit, but I did have criteria that I was relying on. By that point in my life, I had reasoned that the man I would marry was going to be my polar opposite. I am, and have always been, an over-the-top extrovert. I am loud, talkative, and spontaneous to a fault, so I knew there was no possible way I would marry a male version of me. That marriage would spontaneously combust. I was confident my husband would be quiet, introverted, and uber intelligent. So when he walked up to me wearing a plaid shirt and cotton Dockers, with a well-articulated script, I was already hearing wedding bells. *It's him!* I thought.

His question—short, sweet, and to the point—was calculated and intentional. I could tell he didn't casually dispense his words but rather precisely determined when and if he should speak at all. The day he approached me, I knew he wanted to make sure every word counted, and it did. I said yes almost as soon as he completed his big ask.

Like the poster child for naivety, I thought I had all the information I needed to know about my future husband on our first date. I was so convinced that I would marry this man, I decided to start telling people that. Everything in our courtship seemed to be working like clockwork—until one day it wasn't.

We hit an unanticipated mammoth-sized bump on our road toward marital bliss that halted our journey indefinitely. It wasn't that there hadn't been other areas of concern; I just chose not to see them at the time. Like most engaged women, I simply wanted to get married. Eventually, however, I was forced to be honest about the red flags in our relationship.

It began at a Wednesday night communion service. When it was time to take the Lord's Supper, I sensed an uneasiness in my heart. I know now that it was the Holy Spirit prompting me to address an area of sin in my life.

I wanted to ignore the internal urging, but the more I tried to dismiss the conviction, the more uneasy I felt. It became increasingly apparent that a confession was necessary and unavoidable. I had no choice. I didn't want to bring secret sin into my forthcoming union. As a result, I opted not to take communion.

I had been taught to abstain from the Lord's Supper if I had a relational issue to resolve that was within my power to fix. In fact, our church at the time instructed us to go to the person we had a grievance with and make things right immediately. This meant if they were in the sanctuary, you walked right up to them and had a conversation in front of everyone. That took courage I didn't have, but it also took courage to remain seated.

> **Sometimes courage requires a willingness to stand out when you'd rather blend in.**

For years I tried to act like I had everything all together, but remaining in my chair that night was a public admittance that I wasn't perfect. Not only was I not perfect, but I had issues, and they were bad enough to cause me to stay in my seat while everyone else went up to the front of the church to take communion. I wanted desperately to put an end to my shame, but I knew remaining seated in the sanctuary was the exact thing I needed to do. Sometimes courage requires a willingness to stand out when you'd rather blend in.

After what seemed like an eternity, the service ended, and my fiancé and I drove somewhere so we could talk in private. Soon I would make a confession that would forever alter the trajectory of our premarital journey.

For a while I stumbled through the conversation, awkwardly tiptoeing around my discomfort. The uneasiness that comes with needing to reveal what you'd rather not is paralyzing. I wanted to say, "You know what, never mind. This can wait until later."

Dread was slowly inching up from my stomach and attempting to silence my voice, but I resisted and mustered up enough courage to timidly make my confession.

Immediately a massive weight lifted off me while another one came crashing down on my chest. I was no longer dealing with secret shame, but I now had a new concern: facing the reality that my private sin broke the heart of my fiancé.

My sin damaged the trust we were trying to build and broke his heart. It felt like I was taking a sledgehammer to our marriage before it began. As difficult as it was to be honest, I was certain a confession was far better than keeping my struggle concealed.

Secrets only erect a barrier between us and those we love the most. I needed to confess my sin and feel the impact of my words. I needed to own the responsibilities for my actions. I needed to expose my sin and make a conscious decision to turn away from it. I needed to repent.

Marriage, Interrupted

Whereas I am choosing not to reveal the details of my confession, know that my sin was a by-product of never considering myself a pretty girl. I was the one with the big nose, flat chest, and brutal acne. The little sister and never the girlfriend. The one in the shadows of every other girl everywhere. But I was no longer a girl. Now I was a grown woman still clinging to the impact of insecurity, childhood hurts, and an absent father.

I was broken and had learned how to meet my need for affirmation on my own. A woman with father wounds may find herself in this place more often than not. She may be tempted to cling desperately to detrimental habits formed as a means of meeting her need for significance. A second glance or flirtatious interaction with a man both become dangerous and sometimes costly forms of affirmation she may depend on to feel beautiful, wanted, and secure.

Although it was embarrassing to make my confession, it was necessary. I was determined to build the type of marriage I had yet to see in my family. I knew the only way to do this was to begin with a foundation of gut-wrenching honesty between my future spouse and me. We also told our marriage mentors, who advised us to tell our marriage counselors. The corresponding response was something I didn't anticipate.

Our church told us, in so many words, that we were not ready to get married and we both had some more introspective work to do before we could say "I do." They recommended we stop planning our wedding and begin outside counseling separately, immediately, and indefinitely.

Indefinitely was the hardest to accept. Although we could have packed our bags and headed to the county courthouse, we opted to submit to the leadership of our church. It was difficult, embarrassing, and s-l-o-w. They didn't give us a timetable. We didn't know if we would be in this place of premarital limbo for weeks, a full year, or forever. All we knew was that we needed to get additional counseling, and so we did. My fiancé and I became the first couple in the history of our church not to complete the premarital counseling program. We needed additional counseling outside the church. This meant we each went to counseling alone, then we saw a counselor as a couple, and then we received counseling from our pastor.

"Have you set a date yet?" well-meaning church folk would ask. "No, not yet," we would reply, and then it would happen all over again. Everyone seemed to be preoccupied with our indefinite time of waiting, but we had no answers to offer. We couldn't say, "Oh, it will be next year sometime," or "We're planning a fall wedding." I imagine it appeared strange to many, but we chose to submit to a process outlined for us.

We were stuck in a waiting place that forced me to work on the marriage rather than the wedding day. I had no dress fittings or cake tastings. It was just me working on myself. More specifically, I was working with a counselor to identify the dominant thoughts that were driving my behavior.

She instructed me to read *Mind over Mood: Change How You Feel by Changing the Way You Think* by Dennis Greenberger and Christine A. Padesky. This book required that I record the pivotal events that happened in my days and weeks. If I had an argument, anxious thoughts, attention-seeking behavior, or the like, I had to analyze the thoughts behind my actions.

I listed out all the thoughts leading up to the event and then I had to identify the dominant thought that was the basis for my behavior. From there I had to evaluate whether my dominant thought was based on evidence or rooted in my emotions. If my dominant thought was unsubstantiated, I had to counter that thought with a factual statement.

This conditioned me to be proactive rather than reactive in my behavior. For months I took copious notes on myself. I worked on my thoughts repeatedly. It was tedious, inconvenient, and time consuming, but I was willing to do whatever it took to break the hold of the detrimental behaviors that threatened to destroy my marriage before it ever began.

It was a practical take on Romans 12:2:*"Do not conform to the pattern of this world, but be transformed by the renewing of your mind. Then you will be able to test and approve what God's will is—his good, pleasing and perfect will."* The process of renewing our mind is not limited to the thoughts that enter from outside sources. We also have to examine existing thoughts, originating with us, that do not line up with God's Word and drive our behavior.

This process is called *cognitive behavioral therapy* in the counseling world. It's a tool that focuses on changing our pattern of thinking in order to change our behavior. The rationale is that we can't make ourselves stop a particular action, but we can change the thought that's driving it. We don't have to be governed by emotions. We can challenge our emotions with truth, and a corresponding result will be changed behavior.

Often, we do not monitor what we are thinking about; we just let our thoughts run wild and unchecked. It would be good for us to pause and ask ourselves a few questions: *What am I thinking? Where did this thought come from? What does God think about this thought? Is this thought true or a lie?*

I had to evaluate the statements that came into my brain. *My value comes from what other people think of me.* The truth is, my value is not determined by man but by God. *I need the affirmation of others to know my worth.* My worth does not come from man but from God. Countering my lies with the truth of God's Word was a powerful practice for me, but it wasn't a onetime fix. It was more of a lifestyle change.

I still continue to counter with truth the lies that appear in my head, but I'm able to recognize the lies more readily. This is a result of conditioning myself to identify the lies and becoming more acquainted with truth. Familiarizing ourselves with God's Word helps us to distinguish lies from truth. The quicker we identify lies that drive our behavior, the sooner we can counter them with truth, and the less likely they will impact our behavior.

It's important to note that just because a thought appears in our brains, it doesn't mean it originated with us. Our enemy, Satan, is a deceiver and a liar. He can introduce thoughts into our brain that appear to be true but are really lies in disguise. Author and psychologist Dr. Bill Gillham describes this in his book *Lifetime Guarantee*. He says, "He [Satan] can come to you as 'truth,' as 'revelation,' as 'insight into reality.' But how? It's simple. *He gives you a thought in your mind and disguises it to seem as if it is your thought.* You say, 'How could he do that?' By speaking to you with *first-person singular* pronouns (I, me, my, myself, etc)!"[1] As we endeavor to counter every lie with truth we must also recognize this is a spiritual battle as much as it is a mental one. I will speak more about this in chapter 8.

In Philippians 4:8, the apostle Paul tells us how we should think: *"Finally, brothers and sisters, whatever is true, whatever is noble, whatever is right, whatever is pure, whatever is lovely, whatever is admirable—if anything is excellent or praiseworthy—think about such things."* If we discover that what we've been thinking is a lie, we must be willing to do something about it.

> **We can't hurry life change along and force it into our personal time constraints.**

Although my time with that particular counselor ended, there would be more counselors, tears, and more areas to address in me in the years to come. After my individual counseling, my fiancé and I saw a therapist together before meeting with our pastor. Then and only then did we get a green light from our church to get married. The grueling and exhausting work I did in that season of my life was long and arduous, but I'm grateful for it. A commitment to create a healthy marriage required a commitment to do the work necessary to make it possible.

This type of deep soul work is a practice sometimes left out of the marriage preparation equation. Our culture is obsessed with storybook romances and fairy-tale weddings but not the behind-the-scenes work of two becoming one. Intuitively, we know marriage is not about the wedding day, but when a woman is blinded by her desire to experience a day she's dreamt about her entire life, this truth may be of less value. She may be reluctant to listen to the voice of wisdom, tempted to reject internal checks, and determined to ignore massive red flags indicating she's not ready to get married.

Internal work is slow but necessary. We can't hurry life change along and force it into our personal time constraints. Life change doesn't happen on our timetable, but rather on God's.

Effects of a Father-Shaped Vacuum

Before I got married, I took another bold step that could've ended my engagement permanently. In what felt like an excruciating process, I delineated a list of past relationships to my fiancé. I didn't have to do it, I didn't want to do it, but I was determined to walk down the aisle toward holy matrimony as an open book with my future spouse. I could've chosen to conceal my past, but that wasn't an option for me. I deemed it necessary to have the "naked and unashamed" marriage I read about in the Bible.

Naturally, little girls fantasize about their wedding day and happily-ever-after endings; I was no different. I wanted those desperately. I wanted to be married. I wanted to have a family. While fantasizing over my ideal, I also acknowledged the reality that my upbringing predisposed me to repeating the cycle of broken relationships.

Many women who grow up in father-absent homes don't see a healthy marriage between a man and a woman up close. We may grow up in the dark about how a man should engage with his wife daily. We often haven't seen conflict resolution, compromise, and covenant commitment up close. As a result, some of us grow up with father-shaped vacuums and are consequently at a deficit when it comes to interacting with the opposite sex. I was.

In his book *Always Daddy's Girl*, H. Norman Wright says,

> Your relationship with your father was your critical interaction with the masculine gender. He was the first man whose attention you wanted to gain. He was the first man you flirted with, the first man to cuddle you and kiss you, the first man to prize you as a very special girl among all other girls. All of these experiences with your father were vital to the nurturing of the element which makes you different from him and all other men: your femininity. The fawning attention of a father for his daughter prepares her for her uniquely feminine role as a girlfriend, fiancé and wife.[2]

In college I began to realize that the absence of my father meant I'd missed something in my development. This is why I made a commitment to myself to be painstakingly honest with my future husband on the front end of wedded bliss. I wanted to make my future marriage work. The stakes were too high. I didn't want our marriage to be a casualty of my wounds.

I was attempting to build a legacy of healthy marriages and strong family relationships for subsequent generations. I purposed to break the cycle of divorce and abandonment in my family. I wanted my kids, their kids, and their kids' kids to grow up in two-parent households. I was on a mission that reached far beyond my marriage and into the lives of my unborn offspring.

This is why I deemed it necessary to share the shameful truth about my past.

I wanted something different from what I had seen. In my church-saturated upbringing, most of the marriages I saw consisted of ministers and their wives. I knew that the wife sat on a pew at the front of the church and looked cute. Every so often the minister would mention her from the pulpit, and she would grin as the congregation looked on in admiration of their love. It was a shallow understanding of marriage, but it was what I had to go on. This was the extent of what I knew and saw as love between a man and a woman.

My understanding didn't consist of substance and depth on how to make the mystery of becoming one a reality. Everything I knew about marriage was based on what I saw, believed, and heard, but nothing was based on a deeper understanding. Though I was ill-equipped, I wanted to crack the marriage code. I wanted my story to be one that defied the odds. I didn't want to simply remain with my spouse; I wanted to like him. I wanted to be best friends who grow old together.

> **Great marriages are made when we roll up our sleeves and do the hard work of communication, introspection, and growing up.**

I wanted a fairy tale, just like so many other women. I wanted to somehow ride off into the sunset with my knight in shining armor and live happily ever after. But all the wanting in the world wasn't going to manifest a great marriage. Great marriages are made when we roll up our sleeves and do the hard work of communication, introspection, and growing up. Ironically, I thought I had done the hard work prior to getting married. After all, we were the couple with the extra outside-the-church counseling.

I assumed that our extended premarital period (which lasted over a year) worked out all our kinks, and that marriage would be smooth sailing because we went through the counseling crucible prior to jumping the broom. What I didn't know then was that we'd only scratched the surface of the deep inner work that would be needed in our marriage. To my dismay, our first argument happened on our honeymoon.

We had our first time of "intense fellowship" just a few days into what was supposed to be marital bliss. That was when I realized the process of becoming one was going to be just that—a process. Not a microwave but a slow cooker. Merging the mind, will, and emotions of a man with the mind, will, and emotions of a woman is no small feat. From communication to sex, I had a crash course on marriage that required me to deal with the ramifications of growing up without my biological father.

I was a casualty of my parents' divorce, impacted by things I couldn't control, when I was just a baby. Subsequently, I have very few memories of time spent with my dad growing up. I knew my father had a strong accent, a thin frame, and a signature grin. I was aware of his culinary genius, ability to speak multiple languages, handsome features, and love for the finer things in life. What I didn't know was who my father was: his beliefs, perspective, and life experiences, and how he felt about me.

I treasured early visitations we spent together, though supervised and conducted at a family visitation center. What I desperately longed for were late-night talks, daddy-daughter dates, and special times alone with just him and me. I wanted his constant presence in my life. At each juncture, for every milestone, I wanted my father there.

But he wasn't, and the lessons a girl should learn from her father I missed, so I taught myself and took this misinformation right into holy matrimony. Going into marriage, I had a romanticized perspective; my fairy tale included a husband equipped with flowers, continual compliments, an abundant bank account, endless amounts of quality time, and a completely checked off honey-do list. It was basically centered around everything I thought my husband should be doing for *me*. Whether I was saying it out loud or thinking it in my head, this was the general theme.

I assumed my husband was supposed to meet my every need and want. The idea of mutual submission completely went over my head and out the window. I was headstrong, selfish, and willing to fight for my way. At. All. Costs. I entered marriage with a massively self-centered perspective. Naturally, humanity pops out of the womb self-absorbed, but I was a little more prone to this state because I am an only child, an only niece, and an only grandchild. I was spoiled. Rotten. On top of everything, I had a father wound. In fact, I had a bunch of them, but one in particular wreaked a little more havoc than the others.

My Achilles Heel

For as long as I can remember, I have loved the spotlight. I am and have always been an outspoken, never-shy performer. Whether I had a stage or not, I found a way to get attention. But in all the attention and applause I received from people, it never satisfied the attention I craved from my father. I wanted his undivided focus on me. I wanted to know that he valued me. I wanted to know that I mattered to him more than everything and anyone else in this world. I wanted to know that I was special, loved, cherished, beautiful, and wanted by him. Not knowing this left an unsatisfied place in me. A place where I could be deeply wounded.

Once I was married, this yearning for my father's attention was unintentionally transferred to my husband. I wanted my husband to gush over me the way my father hadn't. Marriage was my opportunity to get a taste of what I didn't experience growing up. Of course, I never said this out loud, but my actions and complaints revealed the desires of my heart. I yearned to hear my husband say I was smart, beautiful, a great cook, the perfect wife, and the list goes on.

The little girl in me, who had spent a lifetime looking for her daddy's validation, was attempting to get from her husband everything she had missed. She was an unwanted stowaway on my marital journey that I didn't detect for some time. And she continued to impact my marriage for years.

Whereas it's natural for a wife to want her husband to compliment her, it's not healthy to be dependent on his words. His words shouldn't have the power to define who she is and what she's capable of doing. When a woman finds herself dependent on the affirmation of a man to function, she's in a dangerous place. It's not the responsibility of a husband (or a boyfriend, for that matter) to give his wife what she didn't receive from her father. He is not designed to do this, nor is he capable of filling this crater-sized hole in her soul. I didn't know this when I got married. I had to learn what should've been obvious: my husband is not my daddy.

It took me years to accept this truth. I've made several fruitless attempts at trying to get my unmet childhood needs met by my husband. What I failed to realize is that God has already affirmed every woman through His Word. His affirmation is greater than anything any man could ever offer. Every father-wounded woman longing for affirmation must be willing to make the Word of God our source and sustenance.

My husband loves me deeply, but it's not God's intention for my husband to become the man I wanted my father to be. Inherently, that's flawed thinking. Husbands play a different role than fathers in the life of a woman. A husband should be a loving partner and the other half of a cohesive unit, and a father is a parent who guides a woman into adulthood. There are some things a husband can do in the life of a woman who was not fathered, but a woman shouldn't go into marriage expecting her husband to be who her father wasn't.

As women who didn't receive what we needed from our fathers, we must make the time to grieve this loss in our lives. Doing so requires that we tell the little girl inside of us to pack her bags and leave for good. She can't coexist in a healthy and whole woman of God.

This may be hard to do, but it's necessary. Every father-wounded woman must accept the reality that her childhood is over and never coming back. We're not little girls but grown women. If we're going to move forward in our growth and development, we'll have to accept the reality of what we didn't receive as little girls. We must be willing to acknowledge the ways our father wounds have impacted our relationships with the opposite sex and then purpose to make healing choices. For me, this involved examining not just my thoughts but also my emotions. (This is no small task.)

When God was dishing out emotions, I think He gave me an extra dose. I've always had supersized highs and inconsolable lows. I feel deeply and can easily get lost inside my emotions. Consequently, scrutinizing my feelings is difficult. When I did stop to think about my feelings, I discovered anger was also impacting my marriage. Sometimes unresolved anger with a parent is redirected toward a spouse after you say "I do." This was the case for me.

Shortly after we jumped the broom, anger seeped out of me like hot steam. My husband became an easy target because he was male and close by. In an effort to have a healthy marriage, I had to comb through the tangled mess of my emotions and identify the root cause of my anger.

I was forced to examine my feelings. Just like with my thoughts, I had to evaluate whether my feelings were based on truth or lies. It took counseling, journaling, and much prayer to say, "I'm angry because . . . I feel rejected because . . . I'm hurting because . . ." What I discovered is that sometimes our feelings are indicators of what's right and wrong, but sometimes feelings, though very convincing, don't represent truth at all. Sometimes feelings completely go on a rogue tangent. There are times in our lives when our feelings are misinformed, illogical, and detrimental to our behavior. That's definitely been the case in my life.

I had to learn not to redirect undealt-with feelings and emotions regarding my father's absence toward my husband. To do this I needed to resolve unforgiveness with my dad. (We will cover this in detail in chapter 6.)

These critical lessons have drastically impacted the overall health of my marriage. It's made me less needy, more secure, and a better wife. Thus, my husband has the freedom to be the man God intended him to be for me and not a daddy replacement. I had to choose to interact with my husband not as a wounded girl but as a healthy and whole woman. This choice was the beginning of going to God to get my needs met by Him and not depending on my husband.

Allowing God to Meet Our Needs

I may not know or understand why God allows women to experience father wounds, but I can say God is able to meet our unmet needs. He may use a spouse to do it, a book, the Bible, a message, a counselor, or someone or something else. He's God. What He chooses to use is not a detail we need to know. What is vital on our healing journey is knowing that God, and not another human being, is our source.

If you're not married or in a dating relationship, please don't check out of this conversation. We're all tempted to get our needs met by another person. This is especially true if we have wounds from our fathers. We must be aware of the temptation to make other people our source and guard our heart against it. No human being is capable of easing the pain that a father wound produces in the life of a woman. The ache of a father-wounded daughter is healed only by the infinite love of God. We are to look to Him—and only Him—as our source.

This is easier said than done. People can sometimes feel more tangible than God. We can see, touch, and hear them. I've wrestled with God's ability to meet my unmet needs for most of my life, but I've also discovered time is a great teacher. Attempting to make people our source over and over again will only lead to disappointment. Human beings (every last one of us) are flawed, and even with good intentions, we can't consistently be what another person needs. But God can, and He is able to handle our raw and unfiltered truth.

> **The ache of a father-wounded daughter is healed only by the infinite love of God.**

Choosing to make God our source requires honest communication with Him. We must be willing to be brutally honest about what we're feeling when we're feeling it.

God, I'm lonely.
I feel unloved.
I don't feel valued.
I'm angry.
I'm hurting.
I feel rejected.
I feel wounded.

These are just a few of the conversations I've learned to allow myself to have with God, my heavenly Father. I expanded my list of things God was concerned about to encompass the intimate details of my soul, and over time He met my needs.

Sis, before we were born, God envisioned, fashioned, and placed His seal of approval on us. We are His idea and we always have been. With infinite wisdom, He gets us and loves us deeply. What we need is found in Him.

The truth I had to realize was, though my father didn't affirm me as a child, God affirms me through His Word, and He alone is enough. Period. This is true for me and it's also true for you.

Practical Ways
to Continue Evaluating Your Relationships with Men

- Answer the small group discussion questions.
- Express your feelings in a journal.
- Discuss your emotions with a trusted friend.

- Join a support group.
- Pray to God about your pain.

Questions for Reflection

1. Read and memorize Matthew 19:6; Galatians 2:20; 1 John 1:9; 1 John 3:1; and Philippians 4:19.

2. Evaluate the relationships you have with the opposite sex. Are there areas that do not honor God (e.g., communication, physical interactions, emotions)? If so, how might God be leading you to make changes in your relationships?

3. If you're married or dating, are you placing expectations on your husband or significant other that he was never designed to meet? How might God be leading you to trust Him to meet your needs?

4. Are there areas of secret sins in your life? Is there someone you need to confess them to (your husband or significant other)? How might God be leading you to share those areas with him?

5. Evaluate your thoughts. List any lies you have believed about your value and your worth. Research Scripture verses or passages that will counter these lies, write them on index cards, and memorize them.

6. Where has the father-wounded little girl shown up in your life? How is God leading you to make a healing choice as an adult woman and not a wounded girl?

7. What are practical ways you can allow God to be your source every day?

5

CREATING MY IDEAL

During my freshman year of college, I was hanging out in a friend's dorm room when I noticed a bookshelf in the corner of the room. "I made that bookshelf with my dad," my friend said when I asked her about it. It was an innocent statement, but I was triggered. The words *with my dad* continued to echo in my brain.

Whether it was the preposition *with* or the noun *dad*, her phrase reminded me of the nonexistent relationship I had with my own father. We had never built anything together. I wasn't even sure if he knew I was in college.

I wanted to say, "Girl, me too! My dad and I built . . ." Unfortunately, I had no common ground to stand on, nor did I want to bring up the fact that my narrative was completely different from hers. My experience was on the other end of the father-daughter continuum, and there was no need to change the mood of the moment. Even though her words impacted me deeply, I resolved it would be better not to say anything.

When I left her room that day, my eyelids bulged like dam walls holding back a great flood. My concept of *father* had been limited to a few court-ordered visitations, gifts left on the front porch of my grandparents' house, and Cliff Huxtable. But I craved what she had—a relationship.

Unrealistic Expectations

As a product of the 1980s, my perfect family was the Huxtables, the fictional household featured in the popular *The Cosby Show*. The Huxtables were an African-American family living in Brooklyn Heights, New York. This was my coveted view of family life. They had it all—success, wealth, a clean house (ahem), laughter, and healthy family interactions. Though in recent years Bill Cosby the actor has been in the news regarding his interactions with women, in the 1980s the fictitious Huxtables gave me one of the few models of family life I had.

I secretly but desperately wanted this to be my life. There were, however, a few obvious realities that made this desire impossible. Topping the list would be the fact that I was raised an only child by a single mother in a middle-class household. It was highly unlikely that our little family of two was somehow going to morph into a well-to-do household of seven.

I used to hope that my mom would get married and I would gain an older brother and sister, but I was destined to be an only child. Consequently, while I waited for my television family to manifest, I watched the Huxtables religiously. They became my go-to depiction of what the Black nuclear family was supposed to look like. This was the type of family I wanted, and anything less than my ideal failed greatly in comparison.

My concept of what a father should be in the life of his daughter was shaped largely by Cliff Huxtable. I watched his interactions with his four daughters: Sondra, Denise, Vanessa, and Rudy. It would have suited me just fine if the show producers mysteriously added a sixth child and cast me with the role.

Cliff was tender toward his daughters. Whether he was the doting father or the firm disciplinarian, he was always loving. I gladly would have welcomed either of the two extremes. I didn't care; I just wanted to experience the love of a father. This is why I was so impacted by my friend saying she made a bookshelf with her dad.

I decided to share my grief with someone I deemed a mentor in college. In tears, I described the events that transpired in my friend's dorm room and the way they impacted me. I tried to explain how a flood of emotion overwhelmed me in a way I hadn't anticipated or experienced before. My emotions were complicated. I was grieved by my father's absence in my life, jealous of what my friend experienced, and still hopeful that someday I would have the type of father-daughter relationship I desired. I was one big ball of emotions, and it was messy to sort through.

To my surprise, my mentor had a father-wound story just like I did. There was a season of her life when her father was absent. As she shared her story, I felt more normal than I had in my friend's dorm room. Hearing her talk about the absence of her father was comforting, and it gave me a sense of solidarity. She understood why I would cry about my friend making a bookshelf with her dad. She didn't think my tears were strange or unwarranted.

To my surprise, her story took a dramatic turn. It went beyond the circumstances that were out of her control and moved into how she decided to change her situation. As she spoke about her response to the absence of her father, I couldn't help but think about how I could change my fate in the same way she did.

She talked about writing a letter to her dad detailing the events he had missed. At the conclusion of the letter, she invited her father to be a part of her life—and it worked. The result was favorable and they were able to build a relationship. *This is doable*, I thought.

A Letter to My Father

Eager to establish a relationship with my father, I wasted no time. I now had a time-tested strategy that I could implement. All I would need to do was follow the steps my mentor took. If I could succinctly communicate my heart to my father, he would want a relationship with me, and my problem would be solved. I was naive, hopeful, and determined.

I did my best to include a detailed timeline of my life's highlights. I sat and typed a two-page letter giving the chronological rundown on everything from kindergarten to high school. In my optimistic mind, sharing the missed details would somehow fast-track our relationship. We would bypass the awkwardness of getting-to-know-you and quickly build a parent-child bond. We would be able to start at eighteen and build the relationship I had always longed for. Excited, I mailed the letter from my college post office and then waited for a response.

Day after day I made the short trek from my dorm room to the PO box to see if I received a response. Waiting was agonizing. I began to second-guess myself and wondered if I was crazy. *What if I don't receive a response and I am rejected again?* I questioned. Then, on a routine trip to the post office, I opened my little mailbox and discovered a card from my dad. Inside it was a handwritten letter to me.

A flood of emotions ran through my brain. *Is this really happening?* I thought. *Am I actually corresponding with my father? Could this be the beginning of a relationship with my dad?* I had so much hope, excitement, and optimism in the moment.

I opened the letter and began to read my dad's words. I took in every detail, wanting to know everything I could about the man who had given me life. His handwriting was a blend of print and cursive, his sentences were reflective of his Haitian origin, and his words were intentional. Some of the wording was difficult for me to understand because of the language barrier, but there were a few words that stood out. Excerpts like "I am sorry about everything" and "I love you very much" left a huge impact on my impressionable heart. I had received a letter from my father, and now everything would be different.

We began to communicate periodically via letters and phone conversations. I thought our closeness would grow with every communication, but it wasn't the instant bonding I expected. I found it difficult to push beyond the barriers between us. We were from two different worlds, had lived two very different lives, and even though we shared DNA, talking to him almost always felt like I was trying to get to know him all over again.

In one of those phone conversations, I suggested we connect in person the next time I was home from college. From that point on, I eagerly anticipated the day when I would spend time with my dad. I imagined the meeting through rose-colored glasses.

With excitement, I thought about how we would laugh, share stories, and bond. The day we met, he picked me up in his car and took me to one of his favorite Mexican restaurants. A mix of high hopes and nervous jitters impacted every ounce of my being.

I wish I could say my ideal meeting happened. Instead, I spent a lot of time staring at my menu to pass the time. Nothing was easy about that lunch except eating my entrée. When it ended, I had to accept the fact that even though I was spending time with my biological father, it didn't mean our relationship would instantaneously become the one I dreamt about.

I underestimated the barriers between my dad and me: time, culture, pain, fear, beliefs, mistrust, distance, language, expectations, age, and lifestyle choices, to name a few. Looking back, it's hard to believe I never anticipated that things would be difficult.

All I had ever done was romanticize the idea of one day having a relationship with my dad that mirrored the one Cliff had with his kids. As a result of my father's absence, I created a fantasy father based on a television show.

The fact that I've always been a glass-half-full dreamer didn't help matters either. It only served to further embellish the ongoing fairy tale in my brain. Driven by the ache in my soul, I pursued my dad. I pursued him intensely, believing that my efforts would produce the relationship I longed for. As a result, I called my dad even if he did not call me. I took pictures from my mother's photo albums and made gifts for him. I initiated outings and came up with things we could do together. I invited him to holiday dinners, prayed for him, loved him the best way I knew how, and believed against all doubt that he would love me back in the way I wanted him to. I did everything I could do to build the father-daughter relationship I wanted.

With each phone call initiated, gift given, and invitation offered, I was saying, "Love me. See me. Cherish me. Know me. Be my father." I wanted my dad to want to be the father I had craved my entire life.

What I failed to understand is that you can't make people into who you want them to be. No matter how hard you try, this is impossible. Although I pursued my father diligently and with tremendous effort, the barriers between us couldn't be overcome by human efforts.

This was proven by the numerous times I was ready to give up on a relationship with my dad altogether. "He never calls me!" I said vehemently. "I'm doing all the work in this relationship," I said multiple times. I grew tired of being the pursuer rather than the pursued. I felt like my efforts were not being reciprocated, and I became angry.

> After working diligently to create the reality I wanted, I discovered God was inviting me to be content with the one I had.

I did this well into adulthood, until one day I realized it wasn't working. My efforts could not and would not transform my dad into Cliff Huxtable. Although our relationship improved tremendously during that time, it didn't become the one I longed for.

I wish I could say I was in my teens when this happened or maybe my early twenties, but I wasn't. I was a grown woman with kids before I ever realized a valuable lesson. After working diligently to create the reality I wanted, I discovered God was inviting me to be content with the one I had.

The Father Who'd Always Been There

I failed to realize that while I was pursuing my father, God had been pursuing me—persistently going after my affections when I opted on multiple occasions not to pursue Him back. His relationship with me had been more one-sided than the one I had with my father. God had been loving me since I was conceived, just as we are reminded in Psalm 139:13: *"For you created my inmost being; you knit me together in my mother's womb."* I was His idea.

At critical times in my life, the lavish love of God was overwhelmingly evident. I saw His love in the father figures He placed in my life. I saw this love in His provision for my single-parent mother. I saw God's love in His protection while I was making poor decisions in search of validation. For my entire life, God had been intentionally pursuing me.

> When we obligate another person to fill our emotional bucket, we set ourselves up for disappointment, even if it is our biological father.

While I was looking for love in the male gender, God was trying to get me to understand that His love was all I needed. It was the love of God that helped me see the error in my approach with my father. The impetus for pursuing my father had been centered around me—my needs and my wants.

God showed me that my perspective concerning a relationship with my biological father needed to change. The truth I had to embrace was that initiating a relationship with my father in hopes of receiving his love and affirmation was rooted in flawed thinking. Yes, it's natural for a girl to desire love and affirmation from her dad, but as an adult woman I had to understand my needs are met by God. He may choose to use my father to do this, but He may not. When we obligate another person to fill our emotional bucket, we set ourselves up for disappointment, even if it is our biological father.

Loving with No Strings Attached

Pursuing a relationship with our father requires a commitment to love him with no strings attached. Whether he reciprocates our efforts or not, we can choose to love him. What I came to understand was that loving my father was a choice. I could choose to love him or not. This will look different for every woman.

For some women, it may not be wise to engage in a relationship with their father. It may be better to establish boundaries regarding what a healthy relationship looks like. Authors and psychologists Dr. Henry Cloud and Dr. John Townsend describe boundaries in this way:

> Boundaries define us. They define what is me and what is not me. A boundary shows me where I end and someone else begins, leading me to a sense of ownership. Knowing what I am to own and take responsibility for gives me freedom. If I know where my yard begins and ends, I am free to do with it what I like. Taking responsibility for my life opens up many different options. However, if I do not "own" my life, my choices and options become very limited.[1]

Essentially, boundaries help us to define and protect our soul (mind, will, and emotions). Choosing to love our fathers should not come at our expense.

We have to pray for God's supreme wisdom, and then evaluate the relationship with our fathers to determine what interacting with him should look like. This may mean phone calls only, or meeting in person once a month. This may mean no contact at all but rather praying consistently on his behalf. The point is, engaging with our fathers is not a one-size-fits-all approach. We cannot look at another woman's father-daughter relationship and decide that will work for us. Additionally, we may establish a boundary that might need to be revisited or modified depending on the circumstance. We must look to our heavenly Father to gain wisdom on a relationship with our earthly dad.

I made this shift in the relationship with my father and slowly began to engage with him. This was and is a mind shift for me, but I believe it is nonnegotiable if we're going to initiate a relationship with our father. Embracing a no-strings-attached mindset will safeguard us from expecting him to fill needs better filled by God. We must accept the reality that we cannot change the men our fathers have become; only God can do that.

Prior to initiating a relationship with our fathers, we must be willing to ask ourselves several difficult questions. Take a look at these questions on page 100. Determine which questions you need to ask and answer before initiating contact with your father.

The reality is, all of these questions evaluate the motives of our hearts. They force us to determine whether we're ready to reach out to our fathers at all. If the little girl inside of us is attempting to get her unmet needs satisfied, this is a slippery slope toward disappointment. A father-wounded woman must look to God, not her dad, to meet her unmet needs.

In turn, we're able to love our fathers out of the love we receive from God. I love and pursue my father because I've been loved and pursued by God first. Without Jesus Christ, I would be tempted to slip back into a "you owe me" mentality. When viewing my father-daughter relationship through the lens of the cross, I realize my father owes me nothing. The selfless sacrifice of Christ paid the debt for his sins—and mine too—once and for all. The penalty for his wrongdoing, just like mine, has been paid for by a sinless Savior. Only He can enable us to love unconditionally. This is difficult but doable with the power of God. Christ exerted the same power when He was raised from the grave. His supernatural strength enables us to love our fathers without expectation.

Instead of striving for a fictitious relationship with a fantasy father, God challenged me to embrace a lifestyle of peace. Peace does not mean that everything is the way we want it to be or as it should be. Peace says, "My trust is in God, who is sovereign and in control at all times in all situations, even though things are not the way I desire them to be."

I didn't choose this path on my own; I sensed God moving me in this direction. I remember the day it happened. My father and I were discussing one of his lifestyle choices that I didn't agree with. In that difficult conversation, he made it clear that he wasn't going to change. There we were, stuck at a crossroad, when a light bulb turned on in my brain. In that moment I understood a fundamental principle that affects all relationships. The revelation I received was "You can't change people."

It's not rocket science, I know, but it took me having the uncomfortable conversation with my father and hearing his response before this finally resonated with me. People are who they are, and it's a waste of energy to attempt to mold them into who we want them to be. Only God can do that.

In fact, this is what God did in Genesis 2:7: *"The LORD God formed a man from the dust of the ground and breathed into his nostrils the breath of life, and the man became a living being."* From the dirt of the earth, God fashioned the very first human beings, Adam and Eve. Everything about their environment was perfect and yet they still opted to disobey God. Although God had clearly communicated boundaries and guidelines, they chose to eat from the Tree of the Knowledge of Good and Evil.

If this was the type of behavior demonstrated by the very first human beings, who were fashioned by God Himself, why would I expect to change my father and somehow control his actions? It simply wasn't possible. Trying to change people won't work. It'll only leave you exhausted and frustrated.

Only God is able to transform the human heart. We are reminded of this in the message the Lord gave to the prophet Jeremiah in Jeremiah 18:6 (ERV): *"Family of Israel, you know that I can do the same thing with you. You are like the clay in the potter's hands, and I am the potter."*

Heart change does not happen by willpower, positive thinking, or shock therapy. Genuine life transformation is the work of God, and while we wait for it to happen, we can do one of two things. We can either wallow in self-pity and discouragement or embrace contentment.

Previously, I chose the former as I tried to make my father into the man I wanted him to be. Once I had my epiphany about human behavior, I opted to relinquish the expectation I had for my father to be someone he wasn't. I decided instead to accept the man he was.

Heart change does not happen by willpower, positive thinking, or shock therapy.

I asked God to help me love without expectation—no strings attached. I didn't want to approach my father as the needy little girl in a grown woman's body, still looking for his affirmation and validation. I wanted to come to the table as a woman who was secure in her relationship with God as her heavenly Father.

This time around, if I called, sent a card, or initiated an outing, I did so without looking for a corresponding response from my father (or at least I tried to). I can't say it was perfect. This required me to decide in advance that I was going to love my dad whether he chose to love me back at all. I had to resolve to love him if he never called, sent me a birthday card, or pursued me the way I pursued him for many years.

In doing so, I understood that if my efforts weren't reciprocated, it wasn't an indication that there was anything wrong with me. I was already loved, affirmed, valued, chosen, and seen by God. If my father opted not to engage with me, for whatever reason, it was a reflection of something going on with him. This is the place of security I believe every woman can reach with God's help.

Choosing to love and engage with my dad was my individual decision. I believed then, as I do now, that God was calling me to love my father in this way. In saying that, I don't think this is the path every father-wounded daughter should take. It may not be feasible or wise for every woman to do. Each relationship is different, and no blanket advice applies to every father-wounded woman. This is a delicate road that each woman must walk with God for herself, but we can know the peace God promises always.

Finding this place of peace has been an ongoing journey for me. Before, during, and after I started my blog, I faced areas of tremendous struggle in my father-daughter relationship. This is why I initially kept my blog a secret from him.

For four years, I intentionally kept my dad in the dark about my online writing. Telling him about my blog would force me to have a conversation about us. Like peeling back the layers of an onion, I would have to reveal the motivation behind my writing. I would have to divulge the fact that I suffered for many years in many ways because of his absence in my life.

I didn't want to do it. I wasn't ready to be real about the impact his absence had and was having in my life. I wrapped myself in fear, bundling up in it like a winter coat. I couldn't do it. With ease, I could be brutally honest with the world about topics ranging from relationships to emotional healing, but with my dad I said nothing.

Part of me was content having what I call "weather conversations"—discussing the rain so I could say we talked. Surface conversations were safe and easy. There was no speculation on what the outcome would be. Simply chat on the phone for a few minutes and repeat in a week or so.

Fear was not my only obstacle; shame was also present. Shame reminded me of the various ways I coped with my father's absence, often bringing up my over-a-decade-long struggle with self-esteem, emotions, and males. These were not things I wished to discuss. If I'm honest, part of me wanted to protect my father from knowing how his absence impacted me. I reasoned that our relationship wasn't strong enough to handle the truth.

After all, I had spent all my adult life trying to build some type of connection with him. Despite these efforts, the chasm, although smaller, still existed. In some ways we remained like strangers meeting for the first time over and over again—he, a Haitian-born man in his sixties, and I, his American-born daughter, now middle-aged and still grappling with her father wounds.

Inwardly, I had every intention of telling my dad about my blog, but I could never muster up the courage, until God began to nudge me to do so. One day a thought popped into my mind: *You should tell your father about your blog.* I dismissed this notion as a far-fetched and random idea. But it returned with even greater persistence.

Often, this is how God communicates with me. A persistent thought that won't leave eventually becomes the next act of faith God wants me to take. It wasn't an immediate move of obedience, but eventually I decided to have the difficult conversation with my father.

From the day I purchased my plane ticket to go visit him, I thought about what I would say. How would I begin the conversation, and how would he respond? When my departure date arrived, almost every second was filled with thoughts of the approaching meeting between my father and me.

The reality of what I was about to do gnawed at me. All I could think about were my words and his response. When I felt like backing out, I remembered the apostle Paul's letter to Timothy in 2 Timothy 1:7 (NKJV): *"For God has not given us a spirit of fear, but of power and of love and of a sound mind."* I repeated these words to myself, allowing them to propel me forward.

As I drove to his house in my rental car, silence magnified the moment. I questioned whether I was doing the right thing. Determined, I stepped out of the car, placed my feet on the gravel, and walked down the broken sidewalk toward my father's house. I knocked on the screen door, secretly hoping he wouldn't answer. He did. With a welcoming smile, he opened the door, and my heart sank as I thought about the conversation I intended to have.

Upon entering the house, temptation enticed me to settle for another "weather conversation." I succumbed, but it was over almost as soon as it began. Unsuccessfully, I searched for other things to talk about: sports, current events, anything to pass the time. Nothing was sufficient, and we eventually returned to a deafening silence.

My unspoken words continued to remind me why I traveled more than eight hundred miles to see my father. I wanted to run. I contemplated not going through with it, but I knew now was the time. Then courage decided to show up.

Nervously, and with the awkwardness of a new kid on the first day of school, I opened my mouth to speak. "Um. Well. Dad. I, um, actually wanted to talk about what it was like growing up"—*pause . . . breathe . . . sigh*—"without you," I began. "It was hard." (*Hold back the tears.*) "I needed you. I struggled."

As much as I love to talk, I stumbled through this conversation like a toddler saying her first few words. After talking for a couple of minutes, I reached the pinnacle of my mini-soliloquy and said what I couldn't say four years earlier. "I started a blog for women with father wounds," I told him, culminating my confession.

Whew, I got it out, I thought, but I knew that wasn't enough to help him understand. He wasn't on the internet and he didn't have a smartphone. I knew telling my dad about my blog required even more of me. I took out my cell phone, clicked on the internet app, and typed in the URL address for my blog.

As my home page came up on the screen, I timidly passed the device to him. Silence ensued as he swiped up the surface of my smartphone. After I held my breath for several moments, he responded. Most of his words are a blur, but the ones that I remember are, "I understand, and I'm sorry."

Immediately, I thought of all the times I'd longed to hear my father say those words. I remembered the difficult years of not knowing where he was and why he didn't stay to raise me. I thought about all my challenges with self-esteem, the opposite sex, and my emotions. I thought about the many years of struggle, and yet, in that moment, I knew peace that surpasses all understanding. I knew the peace found in Philippians 4:7.

God had already healed my broken heart, and I had forgiven my father. Although I cherished and appreciated his words, I wasn't dependent on them. I thanked him but ultimately knew my peace was not rooted in him but in God, just as it says in Colossians 3:15: *"Let the peace of Christ rule in your hearts, since as members of one body you were called to peace."*

When it was time for me to go, I stood up and hugged my father with a clear conscience. I felt myself breathing again. I had done it. God had given me the courage to have a difficult conversation with my dad, and I was better for it.

Practical Ways
to Process the Relationship with Your Father

- Answer the small group discussion questions.
- Express your feelings in a journal.
- Discuss your emotions with a trusted friend.
- Join a support group.
- Pray to God about your pain.

Questions for Reflection

1. Read and memorize Romans 8:38–39; Philippians 4:7; 2 Timothy 1:7; and 1 John 3:1.

2. Do you have unrealistic expectations for your biological father?

3. How might God be leading you to accept who your father is?

4. What is one practical way you can love your father now?

5. In what ways has God pursued you? Have you pursued Him in return?

6. How is God leading you to embrace peace?

7. Is God leading you to have a conversation with your father? What is the conversation about? Seek wise counsel before you have a conversation with your father. Make sure you have a strong support system in place. Rid yourself of expectations, and purpose to trust God with the outcome. Set a time and date to have the conversation. Remain prayerful.

Questions to Consider before Initiating a Relationship with Your Father

1. Am I spiritually and emotionally ready to communicate with my father?

2. Do I have any uncommunicated expectations?

3. Are my motivations pure?

4. Do I harbor unforgiveness, bitterness, or anger toward my father?

5. Do I have support in place if reaching out to my father causes me pain?

6. What if he does not love me back?

7. What if he does not want to be in a relationship with me?

8. What if he is addicted to drugs or alcohol or both?

9. What if he is oblivious to the pain he has caused in my life and is unwilling to apologize?

10. What if he is unkind?

11. What if he is not safe?

12. What if he fathered another child and was there for them? How will I respond?

13. What if he wants to keep me a secret?

6

FORGIVING THE UNPARDONABLE

"I don't forgive him" are words my blog readers have expressed on more than one occasion.

I understand these sentiments. Stubbornness runs in my bloodline. I can hold a grudge, preserve it, and hide it in the nooks and crannies of my heart till I need to use it as ammo. I could be a professional grudge holder, and as a result, I'm no stranger to unforgiveness.

I too have voiced my own declarations of don'ts and won'ts concerning my father. Intermingled with an intense desire to know and be known by my daddy, unforgiveness has taken up residence in my heart, moving in and out at will. And though I have wrestled with this state in solitude, I know I'm not alone.

In her book *Forgiving What You Can't Forget*, Lysa TerKeurst describes the pain a person feels when they have been wounded. She says,

> When you've been deeply wounded by another person, it's only natural to be shocked by their utter lack of humanity. It's understandable to wish your life would have never, ever intersected with theirs. To assume the hell you are now forced to live with is absolutely directly connected to a choice they made that can never be unmade. To feel haunted by a shadow version of the offender who caused this, and to almost feel like they are following you around while you replay their cruel act in your mind over and over and over. To feel forever changed in ways you don't want to be.[1]

This is why the actions and deeds of a father can attach themselves to the soul of a woman for her entire lifetime. They have the potential to suck the lifeblood out of her completely, leaving her just a shell of the woman she was intended to be. And though she is a fraction of herself, she is not rendered immobile. She still functions—often at a high level—but the pain of her father wounds lingers just beneath the surface. Periodically, the wounds haunt her like a recurring nightmare, or without warning they set off reactions in her brain and she may find herself blindsided by raw emotions: anger, depression, and grief.

> **The actions and deeds of a father can attach themselves to the soul of a woman for her entire lifetime.**

The Fallacy of Masks

While sitting in a therapy session, this very thing transpired. Not in me—in my counselor. We were separated by a large wooden desk that served as a reminder of the invisible client-counselor boundaries governing our relationship.

Monthly, I paid her so I could pour out my woes like water from a broken faucet. And no matter how devastating my personal accounts were, there was always an emotional barricade—and that desk—between us. She never showed feelings on either end of the continuum, which was fine; I was paying her not to.

Unlike my counselor, I don't have the ability to passively listen to the pain of others without feeling and showing it too. I often empathize to a fault, shouldering the grief of others like it's my own. So as you can imagine, I was shocked when the roles between my counselor and me reversed that day.

On this particular visit I was tackling the subject of my father wounds. "I want to go out on a daddy-daughter date," I said. "I want to be daddy's little girl. How can *God* do that?"

At the conclusion of my rant, I watched in amazement as my Christian counselor morphed into a daddy-wounded peer right before my eyes. My words must have triggered an undisclosed place in her heart, because she bulldozed right through the emotional and professional blockades she had erected. Her eyes filled with tears, her cheeks flushed, and she sniffled. Before I knew it, she was engaged in a full-blown ugly cry, dabbing and wiping her face like it was her session and not mine.

What in the world is happening? I thought but didn't say. Here I was, staring at all of her accolades and accomplishments affixed to the wall, distinguishing her as someone certified to help me overcome my father wounds, and yet she was still dealing with some of her own. I almost got up and bypassed the wooden desk so I could hand her some Kleenex and attempt to console her. I opted not to, committed to the client-counselor boundaries that separated us.

Her response was a reminder: father wounds are absolutely unscrupulous, reducing all of us to little girls still nursing our pain in the bodies of grown women. Here she was, a professional woman and an accomplished author, fixed up and covered up but still wounded. She had an emotional hemorrhage that, to a certain degree, had been kept hidden, but that day my words outed her wounds in grand fashion. While I spoke, she mentally left the conversation and traveled back in time to the place where her father wounded her. Her wounds were so tender and unhealed that they easily resurfaced at the words of a client. That encounter left me with a vivid reminder of just how powerful a father wound can be in the life of a woman.

Inadvertently, we return to the age at which we were wounded. Romanced by sorrow and wooed by our ache, we're tempted to stay there. "Don't leave," our sadness says. "I need you," our pain beckons. And like the lure of a really bad codependent relationship, we find ourselves stuck, addicted to our wounds. I've been here more times than I'd like to admit, and I have plenty of T-shirts to prove it.

What about you? How old were you when the sting of what your daddy did left its imprint on your heart? Two? Six? Twelve? Seventeen? How old are you now as you're grappling with your wounds? It's crazy to think of ourselves as young girls trapped in the body of a woman, but that's who we become when we're wounded, complete with pigtails and frilly socks.

We tell ourselves we can't afford to stay in this place. We have jobs, families, lives, and demands; there's no time for wounded little girls. And so we learn the art of covering up to keep our father wounds at bay. We figure out how to lock the younger versions of ourselves in the closets of our souls so we can live a life void of emotional hiccups. Collectively, we all put on our big-girl panties and move on. This coping mechanism, however, doesn't allow any healing to take place. Genuine healing requires that we grieve the pain of our father wounds; and grieving takes time. Dr. Charles L. Whitfield says in his book *Healing the Child Within: Discovery and Recovery for Adult Children of Dysfunctional Families*, "An ungrieved loss remains forever alive in our unconscious, which has no sense of time. Thus, past losses or even a reminder of the loss, just as current losses or the memory of past losses, evoke fear of further loss in the future."[2] Pretending, denying, hiding, and avoiding the pain won't work. I believe this may have been what my counselor attempted to do.

And I can't blame her, because I'm guilty of trying to mask my wounds too. I believe we all do it at some point. If we're not careful, we may find ourselves traveling through life hidden behind our mask—never fully healing from our father wounds and being able to say goodbye to the little girl inside of us once and for all.

Masks are seducers. They provide so many enticing and momentary bliss-filled options for numbing our pain. We can indulge our appetites, become workaholics, or lose ourselves in romantic relationships. Faking it can appear so much easier than being real. *If I mask my ache, then I can look happy like everyone else. I can create the type of life I want. The type of life I deserve.* So we think.

Besides, being vulnerable requires acknowledging that something is wrong, and who does that? We live in a culture that's too busy for pain. We don't have time to mourn our losses, admit defeat, or handle the obscure places of life. It's uncomfortable, messy, difficult, lonely, and many times unbearable to take off our mask.

So we remain successful, accomplished leaders, but we're still hidden. Our growth journey becomes accustomed to our mask, believing the lie that pain is best left buried beneath our protective outer covering. It's here we may remain—rehearsing memories, remembering words spoken, and grieving severed or nonexistent relationships with our fathers. We get stuck, staying sometimes for days, months, and years. Wounded. Bitter. Angry.

Many, if not most, would say we're justified. Who wouldn't side with the little girl? She's the injured party—an unfortunate and undeserving victim. She doesn't owe her father anything. Her unforgiveness is warranted. I get it, and I'm tempted to raise my fist in solidarity, march down the National Mall, and host a rally for father-wounded women, but God presents a compelling case for forgiveness.

The Truth about Forgiveness

Going against the current of popular opinion, our heavenly Father challenges us all to forgive. Despite mounting evidence backing our resolve to remain unchanged, God isn't giving us a pass. Instead, He gently urges humanity to choose forgiveness.

Matched up against an inexhaustible list of wrongs, this will always be God's response. Whether you were rejected, betrayed, abandoned, abused, or lied to, God says, "Forgive your father." He knows unforgiveness sucks us into its tangled maze with unrelenting force. We struggle, unsuccessfully, to free ourselves but often end up back where we started.

Choosing to forgive is not desirable. It's the road less traveled that Robert Frost talked about. And when we choose that less-traveled path, staying on it is even more difficult than choosing to take it in the first place. This path is narrow, dark, gloomy, and riddled with broken trees and falling branches. It's not inviting at all, but what I realized is that the difficult path leads to the abundant life Jesus spoke about in John 10:10: *"The thief comes only to steal and kill and destroy; I have come that they may have life, and have it to the full."*

This life John talks about is one where I'm fully known and accepted by God. No mask. No faking. Just me and my imperfections. It's in this place that God can begin to work on my ache.

Only when I make the decision to take my mask off can God meet the desperation of my wounded soul. So I selected the path of changing my thoughts about God. And when I did, I saw that in the far distance of this path, riddled with debris, there was a light of hope guiding me on my difficult journey to true healing. On this path, I realized masking our wounds is an easy out, and eventually it will prove ineffective.

> A man can't soothe an inner ache.
> A bottle can't drown a lingering sorrow.
> Success won't mend a broken heart.

These fillers hide and eventually magnify the crater-sized hole lurking within, leaving us longing for substance. And it's not a substitute that we desire. We've had enough of those. What we're looking for is the real: real advice, real peace, real answers, real hope, and a real relationship with God.

Some of us have tiptoed on the edge of forgiveness. Like a child timidly sticking her toe into the swimming pool, we flirted with it. We see women who have taken a deep dive into the waters of forgiveness and wonder if it could ever be us. Can we ever be free from the heavy weight unforgiveness places on us?

Part of what keeps us at the edge is our own personal failure with the subject. Many of us have tried to forgive and failed. Some of us have simply gotten stuck in the process because we were hit unexpectedly by yet another offense: a sarcastic comment, a triggering event, or perpetual rejection. Some of us simply refuse to do it, deeming our fathers undeserving of such a gift.

> **We see women who have taken a deep dive into the waters of forgiveness and wonder if it could ever be us.**

No matter what our experience has been, we know that we ought to forgive but we struggle to do it, especially with our fathers. Offering forgiveness to our fathers can feel downright impossible. It wouldn't be so bad except we know what a father should be and what we didn't have.

A father should be present. He should be available. He should be active in the life of his daughter. He bears the role of protector, provider, and teacher. He is his daughter's first interaction with a man. This knowledge, readily available for the entire world, makes forgiving our daddies difficult.

Often, as we stand at the edge of that inviting pool of forgiveness, we begin to ask ourselves questions. *Why? Why me? Of all the girls in the world, why is this my lot in life? Why couldn't I be the girl doted on by her daddy and treated like the apple of his eye?*

For whatever reason, and through no fault of our own, our daddy wounded us. He left behind painful memories forever seared into our hearts. Some of these wounds were just random occurrences in an otherwise safe and happy upbringing. For others, these wounds were habitually steeped in everyday dysfunction.

And now we no longer find ourselves to be children carrying unhealed wounds, but grown women. These painful souvenirs from our past periodically display their dominance in our present-day reality. Showing up when we least expect them to, they leak out into our relationships with the opposite sex, make appearances in our careers, and influence our self-esteem or lack of it.

If we're going to live healthy and productive lives, we must decide to relinquish our right to hold our fathers responsible for the wrong they have done to us. So the questions remain: How do we heal? How do we forgive the offenses that, in some cases, are still being inflicted? How can we embrace freedom in our hearts and minds?

It would be great if we could just pop a pill and in an instant—*poof!*—we're all healed. If that were the case, I'd be the first person in line. But even if this were possible, that type of forgiveness would be short-lived. We'd be dependent on another pill for every subsequent offense. That's the equivalent of putting a Band-Aid on a gunshot wound. Eventually, our gushing hemorrhage would seep out of that thin piece of plastic.

We need more than a quick fix. We need lasting change, unshakable peace, and relentless grace. We need what I couldn't articulate so many times in my life. We need genuine forgiveness.

I say this with the awareness that father wounds drastically alter the life of a woman; they may lead to struggles with low self-esteem, poor relationships with men, and addictions. As a woman stares these by-products in the face, the last thing she wants to do is forgive her father.

God tells us to forgive not because He is unjustly choosing the side of our offender. He came for the broken, which includes us and our fathers. God can never go against His character and justify unforgiveness, no matter how horrible the offense. He knows that forgiveness, though difficult, is possible for us. It may not seem like it at the time, but this is the absolute best choice a woman wounded by her father can make.

An Unexpected Gift

Three years ago, I received a gift on Father's Day that I didn't ask for but desperately needed. Our family of four had just finished our Father's Day brunch. The kids were happy, my belly was bulging, and the hubby felt appreciated. All was right with the world.

As I sat in the passenger seat of the car gazing out the window, I had a revelation: *I'm not bitter anymore.* I didn't feel any anger regarding my father. I didn't have any frustration about anything he had done in the past or present. My heart was filled with peace and my mind was at rest.

I almost took my hand and slapped myself just to see if I was dreaming, because prior to that Father's Day, I always had some type of unforgiveness residue lingering on me. Not this time. There was no anger or unforgiveness—nothing. I was completely free.

If I were asked to pinpoint one thing I did to get to that place, I wouldn't be able to. In retrospect, I relied, and continue to rely, on several practical tools, which we'll unpack in the next chapter. My experience has been much like taking a trip through the forgiveness buffet line, sometimes going back to pile my plate high with a second helping of my go-to favorites. But if the practical tools are the buffet options, the plate I put them on would have to be my relationship with God.

From my vantage point, there's no possible way any practical tool will be effective without the supernatural power of God. I don't think it's possible to "will" forgiveness in your own strength.

I believe a relationship with God is a prerequisite on the road to forgiving your father.

Even though I grew up in the church, it took me awhile to understand what it means to have a relationship with God. When I was a child, church was as air is—intricately woven into my daily living. Born and reared in the Southern Baptist denomination, I spent many hours inside the four walls of a little sanctuary. This way of life was deeply ingrained into the core of who I was. I faithfully attended a youth meeting on Tuesday night, midweek service on Wednesday night, and an usher meeting on Saturday morning. On Sundays we attended Sunday school and morning worship, sometimes our church visited another church, and then had Baptist Training Union in the evening. I knew the inner workings of church better than I knew God.

Consequently, I developed a belief that knowing God was somehow synonymous with church attendance. Rather than gauging my walk with God by a relationship with Him, I based it on church involvement and mastery of spiritual disciplines. Prayer? Check. Sunday school? Check. Service? Check.

I was a seasoned box checker. Checking boxes satisfied my misguided and performance-based religious standards. My understanding of faith was skewed, to say the least. I believed in God, didn't ask questions, looked the part, and checked boxes well into my thirties.

Then I got schooled by adulthood, which forced me to realize box-checking faith won't sustain me. It only keeps us blind, unable to see the areas in our lives that need to change. That is, until life points them out, desperation supersedes pride, and we find ourselves willing to admit our need for help—which I did.

It was this place that prompted me to pursue counseling and a lot of it. One experience in particular left me at a standstill with God. I was going through a one-on-one curriculum created by my church. This program was a no-cost hybrid of friendship and counseling; an accurate description would be to call it *frounseling*. Each week I sat down with my frounselor at a tiny table in a nearby Starbucks. Sandwiched between coffee drinkers, students, and chatty girlfriends, we tackled subjects like traumatic hurts, upbringing, false beliefs, truth, and forgiveness.

As she helped me unpack the lies I believed about myself, I was conditioning my mind, will, and emotions to think and feel in ways that felt counterintuitive. I was on a mission to create a new normal, replacing thought patterns and false beliefs I had long held about myself. Slowly, I gained a little traction by working on my inner thoughts, but all that growth would soon come to a screeching halt once we started talking about God as Father.

> **I had big faith when it came to the needs of others, but massive doubt when it came to my own.**

Belief in God wasn't my problem. I believed God spoke to Noah and told him to build an ark. I believed He told Abraham to leave his country and relatives and go to the land God would show him. I believed God told Moses to free the children of Israel. I believed in Jesus Christ as my Lord and Savior.

I believed, at least selectively. I believed in God's power to heal the sick, move mountains, and comfort the broken. I had big faith when it came to the needs of others, but massive doubt when it came to my own. Hidden beneath my public confidence in God was a great deal of private skepticism about His ability to be a heavenly Father for me.

After all, He was invisible. How could an invisible God call me on the phone or send a quick "I love you" text? There'd be no daddy-daughter date nights or moments on the couch watching football together. Not to mention, I'd already attempted to trust God countless times before in this area, but my desperate need for a father's calming assurance was met with suffocating silence.

Wrestling with God as a Father

The quote I heard so often in my childhood, "God is a father to the fatherless," seemed completely inoperable in my life. As a result, I wrestled with the truth about God, and deemed a lie more believable.

Like rush-hour traffic on a one-lane highway, I parked here. Pinpointing why is difficult. Maybe it was because of an overwhelming feeling of isolation from God, my own lack of faith, or habitual times of unanswered prayer. I longed to believe I could bypass the mental barriers erected by the word *God* in order to embrace the intimacy evoked by that of *Father*, but I struggled to do so.

I was viewing God through the experience I had with my father. Initially, I didn't realize this was true of me, but all the facts pointed to it. Aside from periodically leaving gifts on the front door of my grandparents' home, and a couple of visitations, my father was distant and absent for much of my life. I developed a view that God was also distant and absent when I needed Him most.

This assumption was challenged in week seven of my frounseling experience. I had to examine a list of Scripture verses that highlighted His attributes and encouraged me to view God as Father. I was confronted with a decision to see God either through the lens of my biological father or for who the Bible says He is. After spending a lifetime in the church, I found myself challenged to believe what the Bible said about God. The chapter that should have taken a week to complete took me five as I grappled with this idea of God as Father.

I had to ask myself if I truly believed God could and would be a father for me. You would think the choice was obvious, a real no-brainer, but I struggled to unequivocally say yes. I was having a difficult time reconciling the God I read about in the Bible with the God I prayed to. The God I read about responded quicker, spoke audibly, and appeared more present in the lives of His people. The God I prayed to seemed silent, distant, and uninterested in me. Although I had grown up in church, this new growth place was requiring me to alter my understanding of God, removing every limitation about who I believed He could be in my life.

Unbeknownst to me, God was simultaneously orchestrating the circumstances of my life in a way that would help settle the issue of believing He could be a father to me. During that season of wrestling with who God was in my life, I had a big ask of Him on the table. I needed a large sum of money to take my inner-city students on an out-of-state trip. The irony of my wrestling is that I never stopped talking to God or even asking Him to do things in my life. There were just certain things I had the confidence to believe for and certain things I didn't (mostly the intimate details of my heart).

Every day, multiple times a day, I continued to ask God for the five-figure amount of money needed to take this trip. I was frantic and didn't know what else to do. My desperation was heightened by the reality that I was not praying just for my hopes but for those of the students I served.

Time continued to pass as we moved closer and closer to the date for our trip. Soon we were a month out with no money. I was preparing to cancel the trip, which would force me to let down my students, their parents, and the administrators, when something unexpected happened.

One of the community members showed up at a parent meeting and said, "Everyone is going on the trip! We have a corporate sponsor who's going to pay the full amount needed." My initial reaction was shock and disbelief. It didn't feel real.

When I finally had the check in hand for the exact amount I'd been petitioning God for multiple times a day, I was overwhelmed by His love. I looked at the amount and burst into tears. Receiving that check shined a spotlight on God as my good Father. He gave me the exact amount I had been asking for down to the penny. That check met my financial and spiritual needs in one transaction. In an instant, I went from second-guessing God's love to being assured and confident that He sees, hears, and loves me.

It felt like I was experiencing Matthew 7:9–11: *"Which of you, if your son asks for bread, will give him a stone? Or if he asks for a fish, will give him a snake? If you, then, though you are evil, know how to give good gifts to your children, how much more will your Father in heaven give good gifts to those who ask him!"*

Receiving that check felt like God was saying, "I am capable of fathering you." He answered my prayer by giving me the exact amount I needed at a time when I was ready to give up. This experience impacted my faith in such a way that I was willing to indisputably say God was capable of being my father.

God used that donation to communicate His lavish love. Prior to receiving the check, I was weighed down by anxiety and doubt, fearful of the possibility of having to disappoint children who had already tasted enough disappointment to last a lifetime. God, however, came through for me. In fact, we ended the year with a surplus and were able to use that as seed money for the next year's trip.

After I accepted God as my Father, I was still challenged every time I felt lonely, broken, forgotten, or wounded. When my prayers went unanswered or I felt abandoned or experienced adversity, I had to settle the idea again and again that an exchange of my father wounds for the love of God the Father was in fact possible.

With stubborn resolve I had to believe God's love for me was not situational but constant and He was able to heal every wound and make me whole.

My relationship with God changed at that point. I began to trust Him more with areas of my heart that I had previously kept off-limits, too afraid I would be abandoned or rejected. It was this willingness to trust in my heavenly Father that laid the foundation for my forgiveness journey. I was confident that no matter how things turned out with my dad, my heavenly Father would be with me every step of the way.

This is why the only compelling reason I have for moving from unforgiveness to forgiveness is my faith in God the Father through Jesus Christ. Jesus left heaven and came to earth not just to die on our behalf but so we wouldn't be bound by anything here on earth—including unforgiveness. He did this so He could be intimately acquainted with every wound known to humankind. And yes, that includes those inflicted by our fathers.

> I'm learning to accept and love my father out of the abundant love God has given me.

As I write these words, I imagine many of you are still questioning God's ability to be a father in the life of a father-wounded woman. I understand the skepticism.

How can an invisible God address a deep-seated father wound? I've heard some women say it is possible to know God as God, but He can't replace the void of a father. In this argument I would ask the doubters what their suggestion is for the father-wounded woman. If God is unable to be a father, what hope do we have to offer humanity?

In an age when one in three children grow up in a home where their biological father is absent, we can't afford to sit on solutions. If someone knows a better fix than a relationship with God the Father through Jesus Christ our Lord, for goodness' sake, I hope they speak up. I invite them into the conversation with me.

I have seen God the Father soothe this ache in my own life. He took an angry and bitter woman and gave her a pliable heart of love. I'm no longer holding on to the wrong done to me; rather, I have discovered a freedom to love the father I have and not the fantasized one I wanted.

No longer am I trying to make our relationship what I used to dream about. I'm not looking to change who my dad is. I'm learning to accept and love my father out of the abundant love God has given me.

Forgiveness Begins with God

So what's your story? Abandonment? Rejection? Abuse? Death? What's the source of your pain? How have you been wounded by your daddy?

Wherever you find yourself, come. God, who reveals Himself to the human race as Father, is waiting on us to choose healing and wholeness instead of a Band-Aid. The journey to forgiving your father begins with Him.

Often, after we've had a relational hiccup or an unexpected meltdown, we choose to turn to God. Whether we come willingly or out of despair, at least we come. God isn't concerned with *how* we come; He is concerned *that* we come. In Matthew 11:28–30, Jesus says, *"Come to me, all you who are weary and burdened, and I will give you rest. Take my yoke upon you and learn from me, for I am gentle and humble in heart, and you will find rest for your souls. For my yoke is easy and my burden is light."* Here, Christ is giving us an open invitation to come as we are:

With baggage in hand,
Tired,
Wounded,
Angry,
Broken and discouraged,
Hungry for hope and yearning for peace.
Come.

God offers us the most compelling reason to forgive. Romans 5:8 says, *"But God demonstrates his own love for us in this: While we were still sinners, Christ died for us."* When we read this verse, it's tempting to gloss over the fact that the sacrificial death of Jesus Christ was an act of love by God the Father on our behalf. Sacrificing His Son was painful. He watched Jesus die a slow and gory death on a cross without intervening, but He did it on our behalf.

He did it so that our sins would be forgiven. It's out of this awareness of what God the Father and God the Son have done for me that I choose not to withhold forgiveness from my biological father. Christ's sacrificial death became the impetus for me to forgive my dad. But I could only make this conscious decision once I had a crystal clear view of my own sin.

As long as I positioned myself on a pedestal high above my father and his sin, I couldn't see my own. It wasn't until I recognized how gravely and desperately I needed forgiveness for my own sin that I realized I was no better than my father. Our sins were different, but our need for a Savior was the same. When I want to stack and categorize a list of wrongs done to me by my father, the actions of God on my behalf compel me not to.

The sacrificial death of Christ Jesus challenges me to forgive in times of frustration, agony, and despair. His choice to die on our behalf is an argument we cannot refute.

He was . . .
Betrayed,
Rejected,
Struck,
Spat on,
Mocked,
Beaten unrecognizable,
Stripped,
Flogged,
Abandoned,
and Crucified,
For me and you.

On a cross Christ died for my unforgivable acts—and those of my father. He did this knowing I would grudgingly offer this gift He so freely gave to me. With Christ as my compass, I must release any and every offender. I found strength to make the choice to forgive because I had already been forgiven.

And it must be noted that this choice doesn't justify the behavior of the guilty party. It doesn't dismiss or excuse the acts they committed against us. Nor does it require forgetting, denying pain, or reconciliation. Forgiveness is a decision to surrender our right to hold another person responsible for the wrong done to us.

> **On a cross Christ died for my unforgivable acts—and those of my father.**

In saying that, there are several things forgiveness is not. It's not glossing over an incident like it didn't happen. Whatever your father did to wound you happened. As a result, it may be necessary to establish some healthy boundaries.

Forgiveness is not justifying or explaining the behavior of our father. We may not even be able to explain our father's actions. They simply may not make sense. Neither justifying nor explaining will help us to process our pain.

Forgiveness doesn't mean that we establish a relationship with our father. For some women, this would not be a healthy or safe decision to make. In some cases, a woman may forgive her father but opt not to be in his life because of his lifestyle choices.

Forgiveness isn't dependent on our father accepting it. We forgive our father because of our personal need to do so and because God commands it.

Forgiveness isn't always an emotional experience. Forgiving our father may be as simple as saying the words "I forgive you." There may not be any emotional release at all. That doesn't make the forgiveness any less substantial or valid. Forgiveness isn't a feeling; it's a decision.

Forgiveness isn't asking God to forgive our father. We forgive him based on a decision we make. Our fathers are individuals who have to establish their own relationship with God. It is not our responsibility to pray for God to forgive them. They must do that for themselves.

Forgiveness is also not asking our fathers to forgive us. If we identify areas we need to ask forgiveness for, that's separate from us forgiving our fathers. Their forgiveness of us has no bearing on us forgiving them.

Most importantly, forgiveness is for *us*. A decision not to forgive will negatively impact our lives. Lysa TerKeurst says it like this: "If healing hasn't been worked out and forgiveness hasn't been walked out, chaos is what will continue to play out."[3] I have the T-shirt and matching bag to prove this. Unforgiveness will show up in our relationships, health, work, and spiritual life. No place is off-limits. For this reason, we don't want to withhold forgiveness from our fathers thinking we're hurting them; we will only be hurting ourselves.

Identifying what forgiveness is *not*, clarifies what it *is*. Forgiveness is a decision. It may not come with emotions. The heavens may not open up and doves may not descend. It may seem like nothing extraordinary has taken place, but it has. Once we decide to forgive, we invite the supernatural power of God into our lives by asking Him to come alongside us and do the heavy lifting. Forgiveness is a decision only we can make and a miracle only God can do. This work isn't easy, but it is doable.

Though I don't know the ache from the misdeeds you've suffered, I know the One who has paid the penalty for your sins and those of your father. This is where forgiveness begins: at the cross. The moment we see the sins of our offender in light of our own sin, we're compelled to offer what we so desperately need.

> **Forgiveness is a decision only we can make and a miracle only God can do.**

When we struggle to consciously choose to forgive our father, we may not see our own sin or the sacrifice of Jesus clearly. But Isaiah 53:5 says this about Jesus's sacrificial death: *"But he was pierced for our transgressions, he was crushed for our iniquities; the punishment that brought us peace was on him, and by his wounds we are healed."*

No matter what it looks like, no one gets a forgiveness caveat, even for severe stories. We all must figure out how to cultivate a lifestyle of perpetual forgiveness every day for every offense. In wrestling with my own forgiveness, I believe a few tools I have relied on to help facilitate this process in my life will benefit you too.

Practical Ways to Process Forgiving Your Father

- Answer the small group discussion questions.
- Express your feelings in a journal.
- Discuss your emotions with a trusted friend.
- Join a support group.
- Pray to God about your pain.

Questions for Reflection

1. Read and memorize Ephesians 4:32; Matthew 6:15; and Luke 6:27.
2. Do you struggle to accept God as a father? If so, what makes it difficult for you?
3. What is forgiveness, based on this chapter?
4. What misconceptions did you have about forgiveness?
5. How have you been forgiven?
6. How might the forgiveness you have received compel you to forgive your father?
7. How has your father wounded you?
8. Have you forgiven your father in the way God has forgiven you? If not, what has been difficult for you?

7

OVERCOMING THE PAIN

Have you ever forgiven someone only to see unforgiveness ram its ugly head back into your heart and mind? I have—more times than I care to admit. In fact, I have some bad news: forgiveness is more of a journey than a destination.

When it comes to forgiving someone, sometimes it seems like we take two steps forward and one step back. I've definitely felt this way. Sometimes, after mustering up all the strength I can to forgive, I'm seemingly catapulted back to the starting line by another wrong.

No one ever said forgiveness was a straight line to a single destination (and thank goodness it isn't). My forgiveness journey has sometimes looked like a zigzag and at other times a cyclical path. We walk this road arriving not at a static location but rather a moving target, because just as we forgive in one area, there'll be more opportunities for us to forgive in another.

Strategies for Forgiveness

Birthed out of my battle with unforgiveness, the strategies and principles I'm sharing with you are ones I've utilized in my own life. I've returned to them time and time again to open the door to my own emotional freedom. I've relied on them to free myself from the suffocating grasp of unforgiveness.

If you're like I was—functionally bound, trapped in routine and rote living, imprisoned by private pain, or crushed under the weight of your daddy wounds—I hope you'll use these practical steps I offer to make forgiveness a lifestyle. Unlock the shackles that have held you prisoner for too long. Free yourself from the unforgiveness, bitterness, anger, and sorrow that have marred your vision. Where you've found it impossible to let go of the pain, may these suggestions help you to embrace freedom.

I'm not admonishing you to do this because it's the right thing to do. Nor am I encouraging you to do this because it's the Christian thing to do. (Although these are both noble reasons.) On the contrary, I'm encouraging you to forgive your father because it's the necessary thing to do. A choice not to forgive will negatively impact your life.

Forgiveness Letter

One of the tools I've used to help me forgive is a forgiveness letter for my eyes only. Even before I had a blog, writing was my therapy. A piece of paper and a pen were like best friends that always knew how to get raw, unfiltered words from me. I would pour out my soul on the pages of my journals; it was a bit of a high for me to fill up one journal and start a brand-new one.

I loved everything about having a blank page to fill. What I valued even more was the clarity I gained after covering those pages with words. There were countless times I unearthed deeply buried emotions that would not have risen to the surface otherwise.

Amazingly, I would always feel so much lighter after writing my thoughts out on paper. Writing can be a healing tool for the most painful places in our lives. When paired with the structure of a forgiveness letter, it becomes a liberating and therapeutic tool.

I've used this resource on numerous occasions, following the steps meticulously as if my life depended on it (because it did). This technique may be helpful for you if the offenses of your father are too difficult to process out loud. Writing a letter provides a guided process designed to help you unpack your pain through a biblical lens.

The idea of writing a forgiveness letter didn't originate with me. In one of our sessions, my counselor asked me, "Have you written a forgiveness letter to your father?"

In thirty years it had never occurred to me that I needed to forgive him. *He wasn't around, so there is nothing I need to forgive,* I thought. I had other people with in-my-face grievances that I was working on releasing. My father, in comparison, wasn't even on the radar. Even though her suggestion took me by surprise and seemed unnecessary, I decided to take her advice.

Initially it was awkward—like penning a letter to a man I didn't have much to say to—but as I began to write, a reservoir of words and emotions poured out. I was shocked. Feelings surfaced that I didn't even know were there. And how could I have known I was carrying a buffet full of undealt-with emotions if I never took the time to acknowledge their existence? Out of sight, out of mind, right? You and I both know the answer.

Sometimes we know we need to move forward but we aren't sure how we're supposed to do it. This is especially true when we fear being hurt again in the same way. A forgiveness letter is one tool that can facilitate our healing multiple times if we need it to.

It's important to note, I never gave the letter to my father. It wasn't for him. The letter was for me to process my feelings, not to unleash my undealt-with emotions on him. As we use this powerful resource, we must remember Proverbs 18:21: *"The tongue has the power of life and death."* We don't want to dispense pain on our fathers in the name of liberating ourselves.

Before you write your own letter, I caution you to not give the letter to your father. If he has harmed you, it may be tempting to seek revenge. You may want to hurt him the way he has hurt you. Don't do it! The Bible has given us specific instructions as to how we're to treat those who wrong us: *"Do not take revenge, my dear friends, but leave room for God's wrath, for it is written: 'It is mine to avenge; I will repay,' says the Lord"* (Rom. 12:19).

Follow these steps to write a forgiveness letter.

Step 1. Write the purpose for the letter and identify what you want to ask forgiveness for. Maybe you're wondering why you would ask your father for forgiveness. He's the one who's done something wrong, not you. You may feel that you haven't done anything requiring forgiveness.

Although you may feel that you are the one wronged and not your father, this is an opportunity for you to ask the Lord to search your heart. Psalm 51:10 says, *"Create in me a pure heart, O God, and renew a steadfast spirit within me."* Remember, forgiveness is for you and not your offender. The best place to begin this journey is with your own heart. As much as we may think we're experts on the condition of our soul, the Bible reminds us that only God knows the human heart. Jeremiah 17:9 tells us, *"The heart is deceitful above all things and beyond cure. Who can understand it?"* And 1 Samuel 16:7 says, *"But the LORD said to Samuel, 'Do not consider his appearance or his height, for I have rejected him. The LORD does not look at the things people look at. People look at the outward appearance, but the LORD looks at the heart.'"*

If we've been harboring unforgiveness toward our fathers, it is highly likely this unforgiveness has cloaked our speech in a way that has dishonored our fathers. We must ask the Holy Spirit to search our hearts as it says in Psalm 139:23: *"Search me, God, and know my heart; test me and know my anxious thoughts."* If the words we speak about our fathers are laced with anger, bitterness, or unforgiveness, God will reveal it to us if we ask Him to do so. To help you with this section, ask God to bring to mind times when you've dishonored your father in word or deed.

Write out the letter below on a piece of paper or in a journal.

Dear Dad,

It has been brought to my attention that there needs to be communication and healing in our relationship. To start, I want to begin this letter by asking you to forgive me. In seeking healing, I realize I must examine myself first. I specifically apologize for _____ (write out all the things God identifies that you need to apologize for).

Step 2. Give yourself an opportunity to specifically list all the things your father has done to hurt you. I encourage you to include every wrong you can think of, every intentional and unintentional offense. Give yourself the space to walk through the pain each action has caused you.

Once you do this, make a conscious decision to forgive your father by writing the statement below. In writing the words *I forgive you,* know that this doesn't condone, dismiss, deny, or excuse the actions of your father. It does not mean he gets away with wronging you. It does mean that you relinquish your right to hold him responsible for the wrong he has done to you and that you trust God to take care of you as it says in His Word: *"Do not take revenge, my dear friends, but leave room for God's wrath, for it is written: 'It is mine to avenge; I will repay,'" says the Lord"* (Rom. 12:19). It's likely that your father has already suffered tremendously for the wrong he has done to you. Withholding forgiveness from him will do more to negatively impact your life than it will his. Trust God and choose to relinquish your right to hold your father responsible.

At this point, forgiveness may feel like insincere lip service because nothing has changed in your heart. Saying "I forgive you" can feel like pulling a Mack truck down the highway with a piece of yarn. The mere thought of uttering the words conjures up every single wrong your father has done to you.

And when we weigh the offense with the benefits of forgiveness, it just doesn't seem worth it. *I give him a pass and he gets off easy. No fair and no way!* And so we opt out. But in doing so, we fail to realize what forgiveness truly is and the benefit it poses for us as the forgiver.

This may take some time. Be patient with yourself as you process your pain. There is no need to rush through this stage, because it may be difficult to do so.

Now add the section below to your letter.

> *I want you to know that I forgive you. I understand that to forgive you does not mean that I condone any actions of the past or present. To forgive you means that I no longer choose to be personally bound to the pain of your actions. I therefore choose, by an act of my will, to forgive you for _____ (be brutally honest about the actions of your father*

*that wounded you). By forgiving you, I am trusting God to
be the great equalizer and avenger.*

Step 3. Tell your father how his actions impacted you. This is the
time to address the emotional, mental, and physical ramifications
of his intentional and unintentional actions toward you. You can
talk about the consequences you experienced throughout your
life. This will help you to continue to grieve not just the actions
of your father but the effects of those actions.

Now add the section below to your letter.

*In choosing to be totally free, I need to tell you how your
actions above affected me. (In this section, list all of your
feelings from childhood to the present that resulted from
the actions of your father.)*

Consider the actions of your father along with the consequences
of those actions and then say how you feel. This is your chance to
say what you would never say to him directly. This section gives you
an opportunity to release frustration you may have been holding
inside for weeks, months, years, or maybe your entire lifetime.

Now add the section below to your letter.

*At this time I need to vent, release, and express my feel-
ings toward you and your actions. (In this section, say everything you want to say that should not be said in person.)*

Step 4. Acknowledge what you appreciate about your father. This
may be difficult depending on the type of father you've had. In
completing this section, consider your dad's character qualities
outside of the ways he has hurt you. It might also be beneficial

to ask God to help you find something to appreciate about your father if you're having a difficult time doing so.

Now add the below section to your letter.

> *In order to complete this healing, I am choosing to acknowledge actions on your part that I admire or cherish. (Depending on your relationship with your father, it may be difficult to come up with information for this section. If you can't complete this section, leave it blank or don't include it in the letter, but I challenge you to find at least one thing you can admire about your father.)*

Step 5. Indicate what you want to thank your father for. If you can't find anything that you're thankful for, you can always be thankful that he gave you life. Had it not been for our fathers, we wouldn't be here, so we can truly be thankful for that.

Now add the section below to your letter.

> *At this time I want to thank you for _____.*

Step 6. Let your father know that you're completely releasing him of his past wrongs. Tell him that you'll no longer hold him responsible for the wrong he has caused.

Now add this final section to your letter.

> *Finally, in completing this letter, I am now choosing to release the past. I am looking toward the future and allowing God to teach me how to love you.*

When I wrote my letter, I couldn't complete it in one sitting. There were times in the letter-writing process that uprooted deep-seated hurts repressed for years. Those hurts had to be grieved before I could continue. I refused to simply stuff them so I could move on with my life. I wanted to intentionally give myself the time and space to grieve every hurt.

Step 7. Read the letter aloud. Much of my grieving was done on my knees by the side of my bed. My tears soaked the comforter until I had enough strength to finish reading the letter out loud. If you can't get through your letter in one sitting, don't worry about it. Healing has no timetable.

> **On our forgiveness journey we must resist the temptation to rush through the process just so we can say we did it.**

On our forgiveness journey we must resist the temptation to rush through the process just so we can say we did it. Completing an exercise with no life transformation is a waste of time. What we desire is growth. We've endured the bondage of unforgiveness long enough. Now we need genuine life change.

Empty Chair Technique

The empty chair technique is used in talk therapy. Although your offender isn't actually there, it can be therapeutic to imagine them sitting in a chair right in front of you. You can say everything you want to say to the empty chair directly that you wouldn't say in person.

Once my letter was completed, I dragged a chair into my bedroom and looked at it. I imagined my father walking into the room and sitting down. Then I looked into his imaginary eyes and read the letter aloud to his imaginary ears.

It may sound crazy or ludicrous to talk to an empty chair as if there were a person sitting on it, but I was desperate to be free. As a result, I was willing to do what might've looked foolish to someone else. I refused to put my healing on hold because I was afraid of what other people would think of me. The reality is, if we choose to write a forgiveness letter and talk to an empty chair in the comfort of our own homes, it is nobody's business but ours. I have done it and will do it again if I need to. I encourage you to do the same.

This exercise lifted a heaviness off me that had previously weighed me down. Unforgiveness is a weight. It is a spirit of heaviness that we carry with us through life unless we give it to God. If we choose not to surrender our unforgiveness to God, it will linger throughout our lives, but it doesn't have to. We can choose to forgive our fathers and take practical steps to support that decision.

You may be thinking, *Why give a piece of your mind to an inanimate object when you could say it directly to the person? Wouldn't it be better to communicate to the one who needs to hear it the most?* Maybe it would feel good for a moment, but after we witnessed the impact of our words, the satisfaction would eventually dissipate and we would be left with the potential consequences: hurt feelings, a severed relationship, and a discouraged father.

You may be thinking, *Why should I care if my father's feelings get hurt? He didn't care about my feelings.* While this is a logical argument, those of us who consider ourselves to be believers don't have the luxury of selectively forgiving others. Ephesians 4:32 encourages us, *"Be kind and compassionate to one another, forgiving each other, just as in Christ God forgave you."*

If we believe in Christ, we have an obligation to be kind, compassionate, and forgiving toward our fathers because God has been kind, compassionate, and forgiving to us. Have you ever received what you did not deserve? Are there places in your life where you have been the recipient of mercy? If this is the case, God is inviting you to demonstrate the same type of love to your father by choosing to read your letter to an empty chair instead of directly to your father.

Even if there's part of us that wants to get even with our fathers and hurt them the way they've hurt us, I believe in the heart of every woman is an innate love for her dad. God placed this resilient love in our hearts before we were ever wounded by the man we wanted to love us the most. I believe this love persists whether our father is in our life or not. This innate love is the reason I believe our forgiveness letter is for us and us alone. We should read it to an empty chair as a healing exercise that will aid us in future interactions with our father.

Prayer

The most basic definition of prayer is talking to God. Given the length of time you've been a Christian, you may think prayer is more complex than that. The reality is, talking to God is that simple. It doesn't require polished communication or articulate sentences. (Thank goodness!) God is capable of handling our gut-honest words and tear-soaked pleas. He hears the desperation of our unspoken worries.

God is willing to listen to our emotional and sometimes messy communication twenty-four hours a day, if need be. Believers have the unique honor and privilege of talking to the Creator of the universe about the things that concern us most. This includes the details of our lives and those of our fathers as well.

You may be opposed to praying for your father. The act of praying for him may seem like an unnecessary service to engage in on his behalf. This may be especially true given the way he hurt you. But Christianity is not a faith that says, "Love those who love you back." Christ left us the words of Luke 6:32–35 as a guideline:

> *If you love those who love you, what credit is that to you? Even sinners love those who love them. And if you do good to those who are good to you, what credit is that to you? Even sinners do that. And if you lend to those from whom you expect repayment, what credit is that to you? Even sinners lend to sinners, expecting to be repaid in full. But love your enemies, do good to them, and lend to them without expecting to get anything back. Then your reward will be great, and you will be children of the Most High, because he is kind to the ungrateful and wicked.*

We could infer that Jesus was also saying, "If you pray only for those who love you, what credit is that to you?" Some of us may feel like our father is our enemy. We may wish him harm more than we desire to see him prosper, but this is not the example Christ set for us. While we were yet in opposition to the cross, Christ died for us (see Rom. 5:8). He loved us while we were not thinking about Him, and quite honestly He continues to love us when we are not thinking about Him.

It is difficult to harbor unforgiveness and pray for the person who wronged us at the same time.

Choosing to pray for our father will impact both our life and his. Praying for our father is another practical act we can do to ensure no bitterness, anger, or unforgiveness gets lodged in our heart. It is difficult to harbor unforgiveness and pray for the person who wronged us at the same time. This single courageous step is powerful and effective in relinquishing our right to hold another person responsible for the wrong they have done to us.

The difficult truth is, we may be the only person in our father's life willing to pray for him. We may be the only encouragement, love, or genuine help our father receives. This doesn't mean we have to feel responsible to provide this for him. God is our father's source just like He is ours. He isn't requiring that we pray for our father. He does, however, ask that we honor him, and praying on his behalf is one way we can do this. In choosing to do so, we simultaneously help ourselves to forgive him.

Scripture Memorization

When I was in my early twenties, I was so determined to transform my thinking. I remember taking pieces of 8.5 x 11 paper and cutting them into four equal parts. Then I wrote Scripture verses on the front and back of each piece of paper. Each day I reviewed the verses religiously with the intention of changing my thought life in a matter of months. (I think you already know my strategy didn't work in the way I thought it would, but I was moving in the right direction.)

The motivation for memorizing Scripture is found in Romans 12:2: *"But be transformed by the renewing of your mind."* God's Word has the power to change our thoughts. This is exactly what I was attempting to do with my all-or-nothing Scripture memorization approach. I wanted to get the unwanted thoughts out and the good, pure, and right thoughts in. We can't change our thinking on our own, but we can lean into the power of God's Word.

We are reminded of the supernatural power of God's Word in Hebrews 4:12: *"For the word of God is alive and active. Sharper than any double-edged sword, it penetrates even to dividing soul and spirit, joints and marrow; it judges the thoughts and attitudes of the heart."* Remember, our actions are driven by our thoughts, so we must be intentional in what we're thinking about.

Sometimes life moves at such a rapid pace and we never stop to think about what we're thinking. If we did, we'd probably encounter several thoughts that don't line up with the Word of God and aren't helpful when it comes to maintaining our resolve to forgive our fathers. Consequently, we have to replace our thoughts with those of God. The only way to do this is to read, study, meditate, and memorize Scripture.

This is what is conveyed by Romans 12:2. To avoid conforming to the pattern of this world, we have to renew our minds. This means we can't rely on what feels good or what the culture tells us is good. In this eye-for-an-eye world, we would be told to bad-mouth and blame our fathers rather than forgive them. This is our natural tendency as human beings, but that's not God's way. We must get rid of our previous way of thinking by immersing ourselves in the Word of God.

Simply reading is not enough. We must meditate on, memorize, and study Scripture. We must also monitor our intake of content that's in direct opposition to the Scripture we are taking in. It's difficult to be mentally and emotionally transformed if we continuously consume a diet that encourages us to conform instead. Some of the content we consume counters our efforts to move in God's direction. Immersing ourselves in God's Word provides the necessary support and ammunition to combat our natural inclination to hold on to unforgiveness.

Counseling

Year six of my marriage was one of the most difficult seasons of my life. Marriage was tough, I had two kids under two, a loved one was dying, and my church of several years was falling apart.

I was s-t-r-u-g-g-l-i-n-g. During that season my husband and I had what I'll call an intense time of fellowship, and I yelled, "We need to get some counseling!"

I meant it. I was convinced that a counselor could fix us. Then that would be one less issue I'd have to deal with. That was what I wanted but not what happened. At the conclusion of that conversation, I changed my "we" to "me" and purposed in my heart to get some help.

With no idea where to turn, I did what seemed logical at the time: I called Focus on the Family, a ministry designed to help Christian families thrive. At that time they had an on-call counselor ready and willing to help people like me. Nervous and unsure, I selected one of my many issues to discuss with a perfect stranger. I did my best to get everything off my chest in forty-five minutes, as the counselor attempted to ask appropriate questions and provide a listening ear.

When I finished what I had to say, the counselor walked me through a forgiveness exercise where I balled up my fist and then released my offenses. After I opened my hand, there was no life change. That exercise magnified the reality that I would need more sessions to process my hurt.

The on-call counselor referred me to a therapist in my area. I proceeded to go for about a year, but there would be many more counselors and many more sessions. This is why I'm a firm believer in counseling. Sometimes you simply need an objective listener to help you sort through traumatic life experiences.

The deterrent for many people is that counseling seems to be an admittance of weakness. On the contrary, seeking the assistance of a counselor takes tremendous courage. It requires you to acknowledge that you have a problem and take action to address it. Rather than camouflaging our issues or acting like they don't exist, engaging in counseling is a choice that prioritizes our emotional healing.

Proverbs 12:15 says, *"The way of fools seems right to them, but the wise listen to advice."* There are some things we will never discover about ourselves until we give someone else permission to point it out to us. If we choose not to, it's not that the unhealed areas of our lives are invisible. On the contrary, those around us can see those broken places in us; we're the ones in the dark.

If we're looking for counseling options, we can inquire with our local churches or the American Association of Christian Counselors. Selecting a counselor is a major decision. You'll be choosing an individual who you'll share the most intimate details of your life with. The counselor you choose will play a very influential role in your life's journey. For this reason, prayerfully consider your options and choose wisely. I believe God has uniquely equipped men and women to help us process our pain and become who God desires us to be.

God has used counselors as His mouthpiece in my life, and it has been the catalyst for monumental growth. He can do the same for you. Although counselors are not a substitute for God, He uses them to help us when we're having difficulty getting unstuck. I can confidently say I wouldn't be where I am now had it not been for the godly counselors in my life.

Forgiveness Wheel

The unfortunate thing about an offense is that it can happen in an instant. You may be at the dinner table, sitting in a restaurant, or at work. What do you do when you need to process unforgiveness quickly? You may not have the time to write someone a letter and put them in the empty chair.

As I reflected over those times in my life, I had an epiphany. I realized that every time I decided to forgive someone, I mentally walked myself through the same steps over and over. This was a sequence I could organize and name, and it was where the Forgiveness Wheel came from. It's a simplified forgiveness process for those times when you need to process quickly.

In saying that, the Forgiveness Wheel is not a magic wand. The act of truly relinquishing our right to hold another person responsible for the wrong they've done to us takes effort on our part and power on God's. The Forgiveness Wheel, however, is an intentional tool that can help us get there.

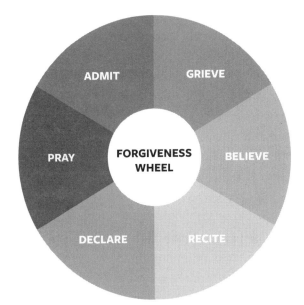

Step 1. The first step is to admit that you have unforgiveness in your heart. Sometimes, depending on whether or not we're in denial, this can be one of the most difficult steps. We must be willing to admit that we're harboring unforgiveness. Most of the time we know but are simply unwilling to acknowledge it. Ask God to show you if there's someone in your life whom you

haven't forgiven. *"If we confess our sins, he is faithful and just and will forgive us our sins and purify us from all unrighteousness"* (1 John 1:9). Who do you need to forgive, and what do you need to forgive them for?

Step 2. The second step is to grieve. After we acknowledge the wrong that's been done to us, we must give ourselves the time and space to grieve. The forgiveness letter is a helpful tool when it comes to grieving. We must be willing to resist the temptation to dismiss the offense or act as if it didn't bother us when it did. *"Blessed are those who mourn, for they will be comforted"* (Matt. 5:9). What did you experience as a result of your father's actions? What do you need to mourn?

Step 3. The third step is to believe. Believing is a pivotal component if we're going to forgive. If we don't believe in Jesus or His sacrificial death on a cross, the motivation we have to forgive won't be enough to sustain us. Christ forgave us, and that's why we too forgive. We must also believe that if we choose to forgive, God will vindicate us. He will right all wrongs on our behalf. *"Do not let your hearts be troubled. You believe in God; believe also in me"* (John 14:1). What do you need to believe about God and His love for you in order to forgive?

Step 4. The fourth step is to recite. We must recite Scripture to combat our old ways of thinking. When we're tempted to be bitter and harbor unforgiveness, reciting Scripture is a powerful tool. *"Do not conform to the pattern of this world, but be transformed by the renewing of your mind. Then you will be able to test and approve what God's will is—his good, pleasing and perfect will"* (Rom. 12:2). What truths do you need to memorize?

Step 5. The fifth step is to declare. Sometimes we have to remind ourselves of our decision to forgive. We have to talk back to our minds and our emotions in conjunction with reciting Scripture, and we must declare, "I have forgiven my offender in Jesus's name. I willingly choose to relinquish my right to hold them responsible for the wrong they've done to me." Proverbs tells us that *"the tongue has the power of life and death, and those who love it will eat its fruit"* (18:21). What declaration do you need to make in order to forgive your father?

Step 6. The final step is to pray. And we cannot underestimate the power of prayer. James 5:16 tells us, *"The prayer of a righteous person is powerful and effective."* As we pray for ourselves and our fathers, God works on our hearts. He is able to do what seems impossible. *"Rejoice always, pray without ceasing, give thanks in all circumstances; for this is the will of God in Christ Jesus for you"* (1 Thess. 5:16–18). What prayer do you need to pray for yourself and your father?

Final Thoughts

When it comes to forgiveness, the obvious person we think about forgiving is our father. There is, however, someone who's a little less noticeable. The woman I'm referring to is as close as our nearest mirror.

It may seem shocking, but sometimes the person we need to forgive is ourselves. Now before you raise your hand in objection, hear me out. Dealing with wounds doesn't come with a manual. Many of us may have made choices and decisions we regret in order to cope.

We may have turned to substances to anesthetize our pain. We may have turned to relationships as an easy distraction. We may have given ourselves to people and things in order to get the affirmation we desperately craved. We may have overdone something, such as eating, working, worrying, or obsessing. Some of our choices came at a cost that was detrimental to us and those we love the most.

Remember the conversation I had with my then fiancé and now husband. Before I could ever bring myself to communicate my past to him, I had to forgive myself. Depending on the consequences, this can be another hard thing to do.

> **Sometimes the person we need to forgive is ourselves.**

Attempting to forgive ourselves may unearth things in our past that we have yet to address. It did for me. After writing a forgiveness letter to my father, I discovered I needed to write one to myself. I cried just as much (maybe more) reading that forgiveness letter to my invisible self as I did reading the one to my invisible father. It was painful to own my behavior, but I did it anyway. I was desperate for a change in myself.

I listed every offense I had committed against myself, including behaviors, words, thoughts, lies that I believed, and anything else I deemed needed to be forgiven. Forgiving ourselves is one of the most freeing acts we can do. This single step has the potential to break the bondage shame and guilt placed us in.

Shame is the feeling of embarrassment or humiliation that comes in response to something we've done, and *guilt* is the feeling of responsibility or remorse for our actions. We may find ourselves rehearsing words, thoughts, and actions repetitively in our minds. This is often followed by condemning thoughts. *How could I be so . . . ? What was I thinking? It's all my fault. I'm so . . . (fill in the blank).*

If you've ever had any of those thoughts, YOU ARE NOT ALONE. I have too, but there's no place for shame, guilt, or condemnation in the life of a completely forgiven daughter of God. We don't have to perpetually punish ourselves for the ways we coped with our father wounds. We can't relive or change the past, nor can we alter the consequences we had to face and may be currently facing. What we can do is make a conscious choice to live in the now. We can choose to live uninhibited by our past and free from all condemnation, as it says in Romans 12:1: *"Therefore, there is now no condemnation for those who are in Christ Jesus."*

So, I want to ask you some questions. Have you forgiven yourself? Are you beating yourself up for past words and behaviors that you can't change or take back? Are you accepting the forgiveness that Christ so freely gives to every woman who wants it?

Sis, if you have not forgiven yourself, know that you can make a conscious choice to do so today. Jesus suffered and died so you can not only forgive your father but yourself too. You don't have to remain weighted down by the sins of your past. You can know complete freedom today.

You may feel like the pain is too deeply lodged in the fabric of your being. It may seem as if healing is an impossible dream. If this is the case, know that God has placed intentional encouragement in the pages of Scripture for you. Ephesians 3:20 says, *"Now to him who is able to do immeasurably more than all we ask or imagine, according to his power that is at work within us."*

The pronouns *we* and *us* include you and me. God is able to do immeasurably more than you could ask, on the inside of you. That is good news! I'm a living witness to this miraculous fact.

Sis, what do you imagine for yourself as it relates to your father wounds? Do you see yourself free? Whole? Content? Secure? God has given every father-wounded woman a promise in His Word that says this, and so much more is possible. He is able to do abundantly more than that!

God is able to help us forgive our fathers and ourselves. We don't have to endure the weight of unforgiveness for our entire lifetime. We can break free from this mental, physical, emotional, and spiritual bondage.

We may not feel like forgiving, but we're not subject to our feelings. Our feelings are subject to the Word of God. We can choose to be transformed by God's Word by applying it to our lives.

Forgiveness is possible because Christ makes it so. I encourage you to use the practical tools mentioned in this chapter to begin or continue your forgiveness journey. Choose to believe that God can and will help you to forgive, and don't quit.

As much as I want to be there every step of the way to provide you with the "keep moving forward" type of encouragement that I know you will need to stay on this path, the reality is I won't. You'll probably feel alone a lot. You'll likely be tempted to quit. You may be hurt again and again. Others may discourage you. Your feelings may overwhelm you. You may just want to get even. If one or more of these things happen (and they probably will), don't give up. Forgiveness is not a meaningless endeavor. Forgiveness is for you and your benefit.

> **Forgiveness is possible because Christ makes it so.**

Although I can't be with you every step of the way, God can. He is so much better than me or your best girlfriend for that matter. He is a consistent friend. He always knows what to say. He never judges or questions why we're in the place we're in. And most importantly, He hasn't abandoned or forsaken you. He is with you always. As you walk the difficult road of forgiveness, God is with you, helping you walk out your decision to forgive yourself and your father.

You may be wondering, *When will I know that I'm free? When will I know that unforgiveness is no longer an Achilles heel for me?* The best answer I can offer is one I heard from pastor and author Andy Stanley in his sermon series "Re-Assembly Required: A Beginner's Guide to Repairing Broken Relationships." He said, "When you can see those people the same way your heavenly Father sees them and when you can feel towards them what your heavenly Father feels towards them, you will know you are making progress."[1]

If you're struggling with unforgiveness, this may feel impossible. If you're solely relying on your own strength, I would say it is impossible. Remember, we're coupling our conscious decision with God's supernatural strength. Thus, the above statement can be a reality for you.

Below is a prayer I created with you in mind. We can call it a jump start on your forgiveness journey. I encourage you to carve out some time alone to pray these words. Give yourself the space needed to read this prayer on your knees and out loud. Ask God to help your mind and heart follow suit. Believe in faith that God will do what seems to be an impossible work in your heart. He did it for me, and I know He can do it for you.

Dear heavenly Father,

You are sovereign, omnipotent, omnipresent, omniscient, creator, eternal, faithful, gracious, holy, immutable, compassionate, loving, kind, patient, perfect, and a good heavenly Father to me. You are my Savior and my King. I praise You because You are El Roi, the God who sees me.

Thank You, God, that You are always accessible to me. Any time that I need You, You are available to me. I can have direct communication with You because You are attentive to my every need. Thank You for being concerned about every detail in my life, including the most tender places in my soul.

Lord, thank You for reminding me that I am not invisible, irrelevant, unwanted, unloved, unimportant, rejected, dismissed, unattractive, or unseen by You. On the contrary, You are the God who sees and knows everything about me. You know my unique personality, my likes and dislikes, my sorrows and my shame. Lord, You even know the number of hairs on my head. You love me, and I am accepted by You. I don't have to perform to earn Your love, but You give it to me lavishly and freely because Your love for me is unrelenting and fierce. God, because You know all these things about me, I'm confident that You know the longing I have for my father's love and involvement in my life.

You know everything about me, including the ache I've carried in my heart for my father. You know every place in my heart that is broken and has longed for his acceptance, validation, affirmation, and love. You see the gaping wound in my soul.

Where I have attempted to cope with the absence of my father by turning to men, sex, success, money, substances, masking, faking, and other substitutes, please forgive me. Where I have blamed You for my lot in life, forgive me. Where I have turned my back on You because of my anger toward You, forgive me. Where I have believed the lie that You're distant, aloof, and uninterested in me, forgive me.

When I'm tempted to return to people, habits, and mindsets, please draw me back to You every time. Remind me of the truths found in Your Word that say You love me lavishly and that You are my Father. Refute every lie that comes into my brain that is contrary to Your Word. Where there are still places in my heart that are broken and yearning for the affirmation of my father, please fill me with Your love, security, hope, peace, joy, and strength. Show me the abundant love and grace found in You.

Please help me to fully relinquish my right to hold my father responsible for the wrong he has done to me. Help me to let my grievances go and trust that as I make a conscious effort to forgive, You will meet my needs. May I trust that You will vindicate me. Lord, when my emotions are tempted to bring up past hurts, remind me that I have chosen not to hold my father responsible for the wrong he has done to me.

Please continue to reveal Yourself to me as my heavenly Father. Help me to overcome every barrier as it relates to interacting with You in this way. Fill any void in me left vacant by the absence of my father.

Thank You for modeling true forgiveness for us every day. May I forever be reminded of the way I have been forgiven as I endeavor to completely and without reservation forgive my earthly father.

In Jesus's name, amen.

More Practical Ways
to Process Forgiving Your Father

- Answer the small group discussion questions.
- Express your feelings in a journal.
- Discuss your emotions with a trusted friend.
- Join a support group.
- Pray to God about your pain.

Questions for Reflection

1. Read and memorize Ephesians 4:32; Matthew 6:15; and Luke 6:27.

2. Have you written a forgiveness letter to your father? If not, follow the guidelines for writing a forgiveness letter and read it out loud to an empty chair. Then answer the rest of these questions.

3. What surprised you?

4. What was healing for you?

5. Do you need to write a forgiveness letter to yourself? If so, follow the guidelines for writing a forgiveness letter and read it out loud to an empty chair.

6. How might the tools listed in this chapter help you to live a lifestyle of forgiveness?

7. Did you read the prayer that begins on page 145? How did it impact you? If not, make the time to read this prayer alone, out loud, and on your knees.

8. What hope do you have as it relates to your father wounds, after completing this chapter?

8

BELIEVING IN THE IMPOSSIBLE

As the granddaughter of a Baptist pastor, I never questioned the stories of the Bible. No matter how far-fetched they may have seemed, I believed them. The challenge began when I had to apply my childlike faith to adult problems.

I had more faith in God parting the Red Sea than His ability to intimately know and love me. I struggled with this well into adulthood. It took more than a decade to realize my perspective was in part a by-product of growing up without my earthly dad.

By design, the relationship with our biological dad should prepare us for a relationship with our heavenly Father. A father provides a window through which we can experience the heart of God. According to *The Washington Times*, "Sociologists say it's common for people to perceive that God is like the fatherly figures in their lives. If dad is caring, patient and concerned then children will believe God has those same characteristics. And the opposite holds true when a father is harsh, judgmental or absent."[1]

Most often, when fathers are tender, loving, and compassionate, this lends itself to our believing God is this way too. Likewise, if the father is abusive or absent physically or emotionally, the adult child may believe that is God's nature as well. I did; I unknowingly equated the absence of my father when I was a child with God's seeming absence when I was an adult.

He didn't speak to me audibly.
He couldn't be seen.
My prayers seemed to go unanswered.
Many times I felt ignored, believing I could never
know and be known by an invisible God.

I was wrong. Examining the relationship with my earthly dad was a prerequisite to embracing God as Father. During a mentoring session, I discovered how different types of earthly dads impact our relationship with God. Just as light illuminates a dark room, understanding the different types of fathers gave me a new perspective on God.

Authoritarian fathers can cause their children to rebel against God. Abusive fathers can cause their children to have difficulties trusting, being vulnerable with, and emotionally relating to God. Distant or passive fathers can cause their children to view God as uninvolved and disinterested in their lives. Absent fathers can cause their children to believe that God is inaccessible or nonexistent.[2]

Lies We Believe

Because my father was absent, I came to view God as distant, silent, and uninterested in the ache I carried in my soul. However, after much introspection and counseling, I began to distinguish the lies that had laid the foundation for my perspective of God. By changing my mindset, I debunked the lies I previously believed were true.

Lie #1: God is like my daddy.

Truth: My dad is like me—flawed, broken, and in need of a Savior. Even the greatest fathers are imperfect and fall short in comparison to God. Although fathers can reflect the heart of God, they are not God, and we must make the distinction.

Lie #2: God's silence means He doesn't love me.

Truth: God may appear silent, but He speaks. His communication is endless; through the Bible, people, nature, and our circumstances, God communicates His love for us. Deep within our souls, an omniscient God engages in a continuous discourse between our thoughts and His. The challenge is silencing the noise around and within us so we can hear.

> **Deep within our souls, an omniscient God engages in a continuous discourse between our thoughts and His.**

Lie #3: God cannot be trusted.

Truth: After experiencing disappointment in my father-daughter relationship, I found it difficult to trust God. But just as a baby begins to walk, I took a step and then another. In fact, I'm still taking steps in my journey with an all-knowing God, forever learning to trust, and countering lies that separate me and God.

Several verses in Scripture substantiate God the Father's role in the lives of His children. Romans 8:15 says, *"The Spirit you received brought about your adoption to sonship. And by him we cry, 'Abba, Father.'"* First John 3:1 says, *"See what great love the Father has lavished on us, that we should be called children of God! And that is what we are!"* And Psalm 68:5 says, *"A father to the fatherless . . . is God in his holy dwelling."*

He has chosen to reveal Himself to all believers as a loving Father in His Word. Despite this truth, many people believe God is unable to be a "real father" in the lives of those who were not fathered by their biological father.

I get it. Logically, it simply doesn't make sense for an infinite God to commune with a finite and flawed individual, but it doesn't have to make sense to be true. Neither you nor I have to believe it for it to be so; it is so.

If the expectation is for God to clothe Himself in flesh and physically do everything we wish our earthly fathers were doing, then we will likely find ourselves disappointed. God is able to do this, but it's not likely that He will.

We don't comprehend God as Father through our limited human understanding. We comprehend God as Father by faith through the Spirit of God who lives on the inside of every believer. Attempting to comprehend God as Father through a human lens will keep us in a perpetual state of frustration and cause us to miss out on the miracle and blessing of a relationship with God as our heavenly Father.

I know this from experience because I looked for an apples-to-apples comparison between God and my father for years. That was the ammunition I used to justify why God could not be a father to me. I had a long list of things that He couldn't do that substantiated why God being a father to the fatherless was one big lie.

When I delved deeper into this argument, however, I discovered how devastating it would be if it were true. If God wasn't capable of being a heavenly Father to all humankind, it would take hope from the world. If we embraced this perspective, there would be women, men, and children who were doomed, handcuffed to their father wounds for a lifetime. They would be forced to deal with the absence of their father on their own.

"Oh, you never knew your dad? That's unfortunate."

"Your father died when you were just a kid? Suck it up."

"You never knew the love of your biological father? Get over it."

"Your father was an alcoholic? That's too bad."

I know that sounds harsh, but essentially that's what we're left with if the idea of knowing God as Father is just a fantasy. Left to fend for ourselves, we would likely try to heal our father wounds with insatiable success, unsatisfying relationships, and overwhelming addictions. None of these things work. The good news is there is hope. The void of the father-wounded daughter is filled by the infinite love of God. He is able to be a father for the fatherless.

Were you abused by your father? You can know healing. Have you been rejected by your daddy? You can find acceptance. Are you unknown by the man you love the most? Even if so, you are loved by God. God is more than capable of meeting your every need.

He is a . . .
Counselor,
Giver,
Provider,
Healer,
Friend,
& Father.
Sis, He is God.

To say that God takes the place of a "real father" in a person's life is too small of a definition of the Father He is for humanity. God can't be limited by our comprehension of the word *father*. He supersedes every connotation. Even if we grew up with a wonderful dad, God remains undeniably the perfect father. He is unmatched in His love toward us. For every daughter desperately longing to know if she will ever experience the love of a father, God, the ultimate Father, responds, "Yes!" We must trust in Him and not the voice of reason. Reason communicates the same thing every time: "This is impossible." The truth is, *"With man this is impossible, but with God all things are possible"* (Matt. 19:26).

> **God can't be limited by our comprehension of the word *father*. He supersedes every connotation.**

Ask God to change your perspective of what knowing Him as Father looks like. Believe against all doubt that you can be known and loved by an omniscient God. Pursue a relationship with God by reading His Word and spending time with Him in prayer. As you do these things, I believe, you'll come to know Him as a heavenly Father.

God's Love Manifested

For fifteen years I was an elementary school teacher for Atlanta Public Schools. During that period, I worked in four schools, most of which were located in low-socioeconomic environments. It wasn't uncommon for me to pass gang members, drug addicts, and prostitutes on my way to work at two of the schools, but I never felt afraid.

Not once did I hesitate to go into the neighborhoods of my students and truly be a part of the community. I felt as if I was respected because of the service I provided. For fourteen years I always felt safe—then that changed in my last year of teaching.

In anger at a decision I made, one of the parents at my school publicly threatened me. It only took a few minutes for news of what he said to spread through the school like wildfire.

Teachers asked what I did, my assistant principal filed a police report, and I had to talk to the police. It jolted me in a way I had never been jolted before. I wanted to pack up my classroom and just be done with school for the year. I was afraid.

Suddenly, I thought twice about getting out of my car. I looked around to see if anyone suspicious was waiting for me. I wondered if it was just an idle threat or if he was really planning to act on it. For a while, I was petrified to go to work, thinking it might mean I would not return home to my family.

However, I had one male colleague who'd been functioning in my life as a big brother. He and his wife had invited my family over to their home, and he had come to some of my son's games. He was a mentor during my tenure at the school.

On the day I was threatened, without being asked, he took it upon himself to move my car to the front of the school. In fact, he reserved a highly visible parking space for me every day until school was out for the summer. Previously I had parked in the lower and less conspicuous parking lot on the back side of the school. His willingness to reserve a parking space made me feel safe, and his actions brought me tremendous peace and comfort during a time when I was filled with anxiety and fear.

I was tremendously grateful for his intervention on my behalf, but I was keenly aware that he was just an extension of my heavenly Father. I viewed his actions through the lens of God. I was and still am convinced that his kindness was God communicating in grand fashion, "I will protect you."

God used my colleague to manifest Psalm 46:1: *"God is our refuge and strength, an ever-present help in trouble."* Although I was experiencing the care and concern from my coworker and friend, I know he was being used by God.

This tangible love of God on my behalf made me feel like His beloved daughter, fiercely protected by her heavenly Father. Where I previously had doubts regarding God's ability to protect me, I literally watched Him do it through the hands and feet of a human being.

I was able to draw this conclusion only because I settled the fact that God is my source. He is able to be my Father. In every circumstance, I purpose to look to God and not man as the One who will provide my every need. He may use others to meet my needs, but He is the impetus behind anything that anyone does on my behalf. This understanding of God is not one I arrived at via logic and reasoning but rather one I understand by faith. This is how we experience God as our heavenly Father.

Just as it says in 2 Corinthians 5:7 (NKJV), *"For we walk by faith, not by sight."* We believe that God is our heavenly Father not because it makes logical sense, but because we choose to trust in the truth of God's Word that says He is our Father.

Saying that God is our heavenly Father doesn't mean forcibly fitting Him into our understanding of the Word. We have innate expectations for the role of an earthly father. As girls, we may expect the father to interrogate our male suitors, tell us we look pretty, and be there to comfort and hold us when we cry.

A relationship with God as our heavenly Father will not look the same as the relationship with an earthly dad. A relationship with God is cultivated by communing with Him through prayer.

In prayer, we remove our barriers to talking with Him, thus deepening our faith and relationship. This is how we come to know Him as a heavenly Father—slowly, over time, as we intentionally and honestly commune with Him.

God communicates who He is in the life of His beloved daughters. Our response is to simply believe. Prayer and Bible reading solidify our faith in God as our heavenly Father. It's a daily, minute-by-minute walk with Him, and it requires a conscious choice to trust that God is exactly who He says He is in the face of doubt and skepticism. God doesn't replace earthly fathers; that box is too limiting. What He offers is far greater: a relationship with Him as our perfect, sovereign, all-knowing, all-powerful, and unchanging heavenly Father.

> **God doesn't replace earthly fathers; that box is too limiting. What He offers is far greater: a relationship with Him as our perfect, sovereign, all-knowing, all-powerful, and unchanging heavenly Father.**

Earthly fathers, no matter how wonderful, are flawed because they are human. God, on the other hand, is not; He is perfect.

Earthly fathers are subject to their humanity and therefore have limitations, habits, weaknesses, and sin in their lives. God does not. Earthly fathers have a finite understanding of who we are. God has an infinite understanding of us. In fact, we are God's idea. He wanted us here. We get a tiny glimpse of God's comprehensive knowledge of us in Psalm 139:13: *"For you created my inmost being; you knit me together in my mother's womb."*

With intentionality God created everything about us: our hair, height, skin tone, personality, gifts, talents, strengths, and weaknesses. We are not a mistake or an accident. We are an intentional decision by the sovereign God of the universe. Before time, He made a conscious decision to create, know, and love His daughters with unconditional love.

This means every time we have ever felt unknown, unwanted, unseen, or unloved, it was just a feeling and not rooted in truth. From our conception and formation in our mother's womb, we have been fully known, wanted, seen, and loved by our heavenly Father.

The combination of our mind, will, and emotions may be overwhelming to our earthly father, but God is not repelled by the complexity of our soul. When He looks at us, He sees His *"fearfully and wonderfully made"* (Ps. 139:14) daughters.

We may see confusion; He sees brilliance.

We may see fear; He sees courage.

We may see despair; He sees hope.

And it's not that God is oblivious to our faults; on the contrary, He sees the sum total of who we are. His view encompasses that humiliating middle school experience; our family function—or lack thereof; and our personality quirks, life purpose, deeply in-grained fears, bad habits, and HORMONES (need I say more).

With unlimited wisdom, God gets us. He deeply understands who we are. He, more than anyone, is concerned about everything that concerns us (see 1 Pet. 5:7). If there is anyone we can trust to handle us with tenderness and compassion, it is God.

The Story of Hagar

We see God's tenderness and compassion in Genesis 16 when we're introduced to Hagar. She was an Egyptian maidservant of Sarai, Abram's wife. Not only was Sarai battling infertility, but she was doing so while clinging to a promise God had given her hus-band, Abram: *"The LORD said to Abram, 'Go from your country, your people and your father's household to the land I will show you. I will make you into a great nation'"* (Gen. 12:1–2).

Then, in Genesis 15:4–5, God clarified how the offspring would come about. He told Abram, *"A son who is your own flesh and blood will be your heir."* Then He took him outside and said, *"Look up at the sky and count the stars—if indeed you can count them. . . . So shall your offspring be."*

Sarai was barren, with a promise that depended on the fruitful-ness of her womb, and nothing was happening. She grew impatient and decided to take matters into her own hands. *"So she said to Abram, 'The LORD has kept me from having children. Go, sleep with my slave; perhaps I can build a family through her'"* (Gen. 16:2).

Sarai was so desperate that she was willing to suggest that her husband sleep with another woman to produce an heir. Abram agreed to what Sarai said, but Hagar was never consulted. She had no say. Her opinion didn't matter. She was not in control of her life or her body.

Hagar conceived. And when she knew she was pregnant, *"she began to despise her mistress"* (v. 4). In the Hebrew, this word *despised* means to slight or be trifling. Hagar had an attitude with Sarai, and many would say she was justified.

Hagar was minding her business, serving Sarai, when out of nowhere Abram comes and sleeps with her as if she was nothing more than an incubator. I imagine she felt betrayed, isolated, mistreated, helpless, and used. She trusted Sarai, and this was what she received in return.

Then Sarai blamed Abram: *"You are responsible for the wrong I am suffering"* (v. 5). At this point, it appears that Sarai was pretty self-absorbed, only thinking about herself and her issues and not those of her maidservant: *"I put my servant in your arms, and now that she knows she is pregnant, she despises me"* (v. 5). Sarai then began to mistreat Hagar, and as a result, Hagar fled out of desperation.

Here Hagar is so relatable because many of us have attempted, unsuccessfully, to flee something or someone. Sometimes life has a way of making us want to escape our problems and believe that we can. We can't.

In this place, you may wonder, *Where is God?* and *How, if He is a loving Father, could He have allowed this (fill in the blank) to happen in my life? Does God care? Is He who He says He is? Is He really a good Father to me?*

It's in this place that we may be overwhelmed by feelings of doubt, discouragement, frustration, abandonment, and despair. This is the place where some walk away from the faith, and I believe this is exactly where Hagar found herself.

Then in Genesis 16:7, *"The angel of the Lord found Hagar near a spring in the desert."* John Gill, an American theologian, believed that the angel of the Lord was the Lord in angelic form.[3] This makes the fact that He came and found her so profound. She didn't go looking for Him. She was on the run, overwhelmed by grief and disappointment, but He pursued her out of His lavish love and compassion.

Hagar was so valued by God that He came and found her. And it wasn't because He didn't know where she was, because we know God is omniscient and knows all things. I believe the pursuit was for Hagar's benefit.

He wanted her to know that even though she had been treated as if her life didn't matter, she was worth looking for. She was worth His time and energy. He wanted her to know she was loved. God says this to all of us.

The angel of the Lord said, *"Hagar, slave of Sarai, where have you come from, and where are you going?"* (v. 8). This interaction was so intimate. He pursued her, He engaged with her, and He listened to her. She responded, *"I'm running away from my mistress Sarai"* (v. 8).

The angel of the Lord then instructed her, *"Go back to your mistress and submit to her"* (v. 9). This isn't what we expected, nor is it what any of us want to hear. We envision God the Father as a rescuer. He's supposed to swoop down like Superman and remove everything bad from our lives. He's supposed to save us from our plights and instantaneously make all things wonderful and new, but here we see that this wasn't God's plan. This isn't to say that God won't rescue us, but it is to say that it may not be His plan.

He didn't say to Hagar, "I'll get you out of this situation," or, "I'll get you a place of your own, and you'll raise your son there." He said, "I will bless you in the midst of your place of pain. Go back to your mistress."

The angel of the Lord promised Hagar, *"I will so increase your descendants that they will be too numerous to count"* (v. 10). He was essentially saying, "I'm going to bless you in the place where you feel isolated, abandoned, broken, and trapped." God didn't change her circumstance; He opted to bless her in the midst of it.

As a result, *"She gave this name to the LORD who spoke to her: 'You are the God who sees me,' for she said, 'I have now seen the One who sees me'"* (v. 13). What Hagar desperately needed was to be seen. She needed to know that she was not invisible. The deep longing of her heart was to know that someone saw her plight and cared. She found this in God, and in return she gave Him the name El Roi, meaning "the One who sees."

Hagar reminds us all of God's tangible love when we are suffering, isolated, broken, or abandoned. Though we may feel this way, it's not an indication of God's absence in our lives or lack of love for us. God is still El Roi, the God who sees, wherever we may find ourselves today.

I was reminded of another truth about Genesis 16:13 in a Bible study. A fact that is sometimes overlooked is that not only did God see Hagar, but Hagar saw God seeing her. There was a time in my life when I felt unseen by God and He was simultaneously unseen by me. I couldn't see glimpses of Him working in my life, but He was there.

Here Hagar said, "Even though life is hard, I see God seeing me. Even though I have been mistreated by my mistress, I see God seeing me. Even though I'm scared and broken, I see God seeing me."

Sis, God sees you right now, but do you see Him? If you take a step back, can you see His divine intervention in your place of pain? I believe the God who came and pursued Hagar is pursuing us as well. It's in His nature to pursue us, and His attributes don't change no matter what He allows us to experience. Sometimes the presence of pain in our lives causes us to question God as a good Father—because what type of father would watch his children suffer?

There are many reasons why God allows suffering in our lives. It could be for spiritual growth: *"Let perseverance finish its work so that you may be mature and complete, not lacking anything"* (James 1:4). It could be for correction: *"Because the Lord disciplines the one he loves, and he chastens everyone he accepts as his son"* (Heb. 12:6). It could just be a part of the Christian walk: *"I have been crucified with Christ and I no longer live, but Christ lives in me. The life I now live in the body, I live by faith in the Son of God, who loved me and gave himself for me"* (Gal. 2:20).

Painful circumstances do not negate who God is.

Sis, knowing God as Father means we understand He is not Superman keeping us from experiencing pain, nor is He a cruel dictator. He is God, and His attributes are immutable even when we experience painful circumstances. In the story of Hagar we see several of God's unchanging attributes.

God is personable and intentional. In Genesis 16:7, He went and found Hagar for her benefit. He finds us through podcasts, messages, books, radio, encouragement from a friend, a Bible study, His Word, and so much more. God is relentless in His pursuit of us.

God is attentive and compassionate. In Genesis 16:8, He listened to Hagar. He listens to our every cry, concern, gripe, and prayer. God is ready and fully capable of handling our gut-honest thoughts and feelings.

God is a giver of good gifts. In Genesis 16:9, He blessed Hagar in the midst of her difficulties. Sometimes God will swoop in, save the day, and rescue us, but sometimes He chooses to sustain us right where we are.

God is a restorer. In Genesis 16:10, He restored Hagar. Through no fault of her own, Hagar had her dignity stripped from her. She may have been robbed of her virginity and used by her mistress, but God restored her dignity through the promise of many descendants who would be too numerous to count. God can take the painful circumstances that He allows in our lives and turn them around for our good.

> **God is relentless in His pursuit of us.**

God is a caring heavenly Father. In Genesis 16:13, Hagar calls God by the name El Roi. No matter where we find ourselves in life, we can be certain that the God who created the entire world sees us. He loves us and is intimately concerned about the details of our lives. Though suffering exists, God's love is evident in the midst of it.

My journey to see God as the perfect Father was done reluctantly. God wasn't my first, second, or third choice; He was my last resort. Had I thoroughly researched His unchanging character, I would have come to the conclusion that God is the only father who is perfect 100 percent of the time. Below are just a few attributes of God.

- Loving (sacrificial)—John 3:16
- Disciplining—Proverbs 3:11–12
- Caring—1 Peter 5:7
- Available—Psalm 139:1–12
- Knowledgeable—Romans 11:33–34
- Giving—Matthew 7:7–11
- Encouraging—Philippians 4:13

- Loving (unconditional)—1 John 4:8
- Not easily angered—Psalm 103:8
- Selfless—John 15:13
- Adoring—Psalm 139:13–18
- Optimistic—1 Corinthians 13:7
- Protecting—1 Corinthians 13:7; Psalm 46:1
- Providing—Philippians 4:19
- Courageous—1 John 4:18
- Strong—2 Corinthians 12:9

God can't be limited by our comprehension of the word *father*, because He supersedes every connotation of the word. He never changes, His love is unconditional, and His ways are incomprehensible.

Whether your earthly father was good, horrible, or somewhere in between, God, our heavenly Father, is in a category all His own. He is the bona fide rock that I've come to depend on. Just as God has proven to be a father in my life, I believe He longs to be that in yours. If you, like me, have clung tightly to an imaginary dad, I encourage you to let go of your fantasy father and embrace a real relationship with almighty God. If you've been reluctant to give God all of your heart, fearing you would just end up disappointed, go ahead and trust Him to be who He says He is in your life.

The Unseen Plot

My aunt introduced me to my first mystery television series. It was a ritual of hers to fall asleep watching back-to-back episodes of *Perry Mason* every night. *Perry Mason* was the 1950s TV series that centered around a criminal defense attorney who proved his client's innocence by finding the real murderer.

Early introduction to this black-and-white classic cultivated a love for mysteries in me. I prided myself on being able to figure out whodunit before the murderer was revealed on television. Eventually, I graduated to other shows like *Matlock*, *Moonlighting*, and *CSI*, improving my amateur detective skills along the way. As confident as I am with my gumshoe skills, sometimes I am completely stumped and blindsided when the criminal is exposed.

The evidence points toward one character while the murderer hides in plain sight. He has an alibi. There is no obvious motive. No one suspects it's him. Then the plot unfolds, and I discover I didn't have everything figured out like I thought I did.

I've had a similar revelation when it comes to father wounds. Our biological father appears to be the primary person responsible for our pain. It's obvious. But what if our father is a victim and not the bad guy? What if there is a master plan that we have not entertained? What if the events that have transpired between us and our fathers are just smokescreens disguising a plan set in motion before we were born? What if the guilty party is hiding in plain sight?

I am convinced the prime suspect we often overlook is our unseen enemy, Satan. He was once known as Lucifer prior to becoming corrupted and filled with pride on account of his beauty (Ezek. 28:17). As a result, the devil became an enemy of God.

For those of us who consider ourselves followers of Jesus Christ, the devil is our enemy as well. We are reminded of this in 1 Peter 5:8, *"Be alert and of sober mind. Your enemy the devil prowls around like a roaring lion looking for someone to devour."* It is important to note that he prowls around "like a roaring lion" but he is not one. Then in Ephesians 6:12, it says, *"For our struggle is not against flesh and blood, but against the rulers, against the authorities, against the powers of this dark world and against the spiritual forces of evil in the heavenly realms."* We have a very real enemy, and it is not our biological father.

The devil is known as a deceiver (2 Cor. 11:14) and a liar and a murderer (John 8:44), among other descriptions. He is relentless and unscrupulous in his attacks. He will do anything to separate humanity from God. Nothing is off-limits—not our memories, thoughts, bodies, or even our father-daughter relationships.

In fact, because God has chosen to reveal Himself to humanity as a Father, I believe the devil intentionally attacks the relationship between fathers and their children. By targeting the father, the devil singlehandedly creates a snowball of consequences that will continue to wreak havoc on future generations.

When the devil attacks fathers, he places a bull's-eye on the family unit, the primary vehicle God uses to perpetuate a godly legacy. This is where God teaches us about His nature, unconditional love, discipline, forgiveness, marriage, relationships, and so much more. When Satan attacks the father, he renders a devastating blow to God's design for the family, resulting in far-reaching spiritual and natural consequences. According to the National Fatherhood Initiative, when a child grows up in a father-absent home, they are

- Four times at greater risk of poverty.
- More likely to have behavioral problems.
- More likely to go to prison.
- More likely to commit a crime.
- Seven times more likely to get pregnant as a teen.
- More likely to face abuse and neglect.

- More likely to abuse drugs and alcohol.
- Two times more likely to suffer obesity.
- Two times more likely to drop out of school.[4]

Highlighting the influence of our adversary, the devil, does not negate the responsibilities of our fathers, but it does give us additional perspective when thinking about our father wounds. There are unseen forces at work. Our fathers are victims too. Many of them were not fathered themselves. They were abused, neglected, unloved, and unfathered. The wounds they knowingly and unknowingly inflict on their daughters are likely by-products of their own wounds.

If the love of God does not penetrate their hearts, they may die not knowing His unconditional love for them. If they have succumbed to the problems that led to our father wounds—adultery, addiction, selfishness, pride, divorce, abandonment, abuse, silence, or incarceration—they are right where the devil wants them to be: broken, hurting, blinded, and lost.

God does not discriminate. He extends an invitation to us and our biological fathers to know Him as the ultimate Father. He enables us to be victorious over our enemy, the devil, as it says in Revelation 12:11: *They triumphed over him by the blood of the Lamb and by the word of their testimony; they did not love their lives so much as to shrink from death.*

The devil's elaborate plan to destroy the family will not prevail. He is a defeated foe. In Christ we will overcome our wounds. No matter what our biological father has done, he is not our enemy. The devil is, and he does not want us to experience the peace that comes from embracing God as our heavenly Father. We must resist the temptation to allow our relationship with our biological father to create a barrier to knowing God as our heavenly One.

Practical Ways
to Know God as Father

- Answer the small group discussion questions.
- Express your feelings in a journal.
- Discuss your emotions with a trusted friend.
- Join a support group.
- Pray to God about your pain.

Questions for Reflection

1. Read and memorize 2 Corinthians 5:7; Romans 8:15; 1 John 3:1; and Psalm 68:5.
2. Do you consider God your heavenly Father? Why or why not?
3. If you answered no, how might God be leading you to embrace Him as a father?
4. If you answered no, what practical steps can you take to build a relationship with God as your Father?
5. What peace does knowing God as Father offer you?
6. How have you seen the devil at work in your father-daughter relationship? How might the realization of the devil as our enemy impact your perspective and approach to your father?

MAKING PEACE
WITH THE PRESENT

I wanted to get everything right when I was pregnant with my first son. I meticulously read *What to Expect When You're Expecting*, took my prenatal vitamins, read books to my unborn baby, and went to Lamaze classes. My husband and I were more than equipped with classical music CDs, white noise, and every newborn invention available in Babies"R"Us.

We were going to be the perfect parents—and then my son was born. Things were going great until we brought him home and I realized parenting is anything but perfect. For starters, my nurse team that helped me go to the bathroom, brought me food, and bathed the baby didn't make home visits. This was on top of my getting adjusted to my new body—complete with breast engorgement, cellulite, stitches, and soreness.

As prepared as my husband and I thought we were, there were so many things we hadn't thought about. Somehow, non-negotiables like eating and grocery shopping slipped my mind. Exhaustion made simple tasks seem impossible to complete. Laundry piled up, regular home maintenance went undone, my husband went back to work, and it didn't take me long to realize we weren't going to be perfect parents. We were going to do the best we could.

The other little detail I failed to consider was the fact that life's challenges are only magnified with a baby. If I was having an issue in my marriage, or with working, pooping, processing childhood hurt, attempting to heal, or just trying to grow and change, it all had to happen while raising a tiny, crying, dependent human being. At no point in life are you given the option to sit your parenting hat on the counter while you get yourself together. Whatever journey you go through as an individual, your children are right there with you asking you to meet their needs and wants over and over again.

Parenting humbled me. The unfounded pride I had going into the parenting game was reduced to a desperate dependence on God. I had to learn to give myself grace for not being the Pinterest-perfect mother I thought I would be: taking milestone pictures like clockwork, baking cookies, and always having a clean house (insert sigh). There were days when I got things right, but there were many days when things went terribly wrong. My weaknesses inadvertently short-circuited my desire to be a perfect parent.

An example would be the time my younger son was burned by a hot iron as a toddler. (You know it's bad when the preschool teacher asks if you were contacted by Child Protective Services.) Then there were the times when my children accidentally rolled down the stairs, almost drowned, ate seaweed and sand, and had to fend for themselves for breakfast, lunch, and dinner.

I could fill a book with all my parenting blunders, and I'm pretty confident that my kids are going to need a little counseling when they are grown. These shameful truths don't make me a bad mother, but they do make me human. When we become parents, our hang-ups, bad habits, and character flaws don't magically disappear. We don't immediately become more mature and responsible people. On the contrary, parenting is likely to amplify every weakness we have, causing us to question whether we have what it takes to get a child from birth to eighteen in one piece.

We need God if we're to parent well despite our humanity. Failure taught me this. In the process, I've also learned to give my imperfect-parenting self some grace because, no matter how well-intentioned I am, I'm going to blow it from time to time.

It's taken me years to realize the same grace I had to afford myself as a mom also needed to be extended to my own parents. Hear me out. They too are human, with flaws, sin patterns, insecurities, inconsistencies, and weaknesses (just like me). It should be noted that grace is not a dismissal or a denial of what has been done. Grace is a choice to offer allowances—sometimes undeserved—for failures, mistakes, and wrongdoing.

Father Wounds in Family Lines

A few years ago, I was attending a church service with my mother when the minister asked, "How many of you never heard your biological father say I love you?" I sheepishly raised my hand and looked around the room, only to turn to my right and discover my mother's hand was raised also.

What? I thought. In the thirty years of my life, my mother had never communicated this fact to me. And how could she if the topic never came up? From my limited grandchild vantage point, my grandfather had no flaws. That experience, however, opened up a candid conversation with my mom about who he was as a father.

I learned that although my grandfather was a great man, he wasn't an affectionate father. He didn't play checkers with his girls, take them on daddy-daughter dates, or teach them what to look for in a potential husband. This fact didn't take anything away from who I thought he was, but it does make him more human. More flawed. This is why when my mom met my father, she had a limited understanding of what it took to make a marriage work.

Warm sands and beautiful beaches characterized the landscape my parents looked at from the Norwegian cruise ship where they met. My mother was on a girls' trip, and my father was the waiter assigned to their table. With charm, handsome features, and culinary expertise, my dad served my mother and her group of friends for every meal. Somewhere between the ship's departure and return to the States, my parents started a relationship. After the cruise ended, they corresponded by writing letters until my father's tenure on the ship ended.

He then moved to the United States and they were married in the living room of my grandparents' home. It may sound romantic, but their marriage was short-lived and they divorced not long after they were married. What my mom didn't realize prior to marrying my father was that she, like me, had father wounds. Unbeknownst to her, my father did too. My dad had spent only a little time with his father before he died of a massive heart attack, leaving my father to discover how to become a man on his own.

Author and pastor T. D. Jakes talks about boys who lose their father prematurely in his book *He-Motions: Strength for Men, Solutions for Women*. He says, "Without the legacy of fatherhood, many men today are at a loss as to how to fulfill that role. The mere passage of time takes a boy and makes him grow, but he has no guidance in how to become a man. Biology enables him to make babies, but he has no idea how to father them."[1]

Stephen Arterburn echoes these sentiments in *The Secrets Men Keep*. He says,

> There are millions of walking wounded men in our culture who never received from their fathers the love, truth, and affirmation they needed. They were raised by fathers who were raised by fathers who were raised by fathers . . . who were not equipped to reproduce healthy and whole young adults and release them into the world. There are open wounds and sores that must be healed and closure that must be gained in order for the cycle of dysfunction to be stopped. Men who are not loved by their fathers cannot love their own children.[2]

My father carried the wound of losing his dad throughout his life. I believe it was a loss he couldn't shake and a wound he would continue to process long after I was born. In saying that, a father's father wounds do not justify him wounding his children, but they do offer a new perspective. They give us another lens through which to view our fathers. Thus, we're enabled to see our fathers as human beings with their own set of hurts to overcome. Though it seems logical to expect a father to father his children, he simply may not have the tools needed to do it. Expecting him to give what he didn't receive will lead to disappointment. This was something neither my mom nor my dad recognized prior to getting married.

Before my mom and dad said "I do," there was no group or one-on-one premarital counseling, no married couple seminars, and no self-help marriage books. They simply took the leap and dealt with the consequences. They weren't ready for marriage.

Once they became one, the father wounds of both my mother and father negatively impacted their relationship.

It didn't take long for them to realize they were unequally yoked. My father, who was from another country and culture, was ten years my mother's junior and developed an addiction to alcohol that would eventually impact much of his life and most of mine. My mother was expecting the fairy tale, naively assuming when you get married you naturally live happily ever after. Consequently, they divorced not long after they married, but not before they had me.

I was born into a broken home. My mother raised me the best she knew how while attempting to process her own pain and shattered dreams. My father did the same, although his struggles with alcohol often came with costly results.

> **God specializes in less-than-ideal circumstances. He takes the raw materials of our lives and makes a beautiful display of who He is able to be for all humanity.**

Nothing about my entrance into this world was ideal, and if you look at the statistics for children born into situations like mine, they're not good. The statistics from the U.S. Census Bureau indicate I was seven times more likely to become a teenage mother. Four times more likely to live in poverty. Two times more likely to drop out of high school, and more likely to abuse alcohol and drugs.[3] According to the statistics, the current facts of my life feel like a miracle, but I'm convinced that God specializes in less-than-ideal circumstances. He takes the raw materials of our lives and makes a beautiful display of who He is able to be for all humanity.

Finding Contentment in God

This was the case for Leah, who was placed into a polygamous marriage by her father. Hers was a less-than-ideal marriage that continued to get worse. Everyone suffered. Leah suffered because she married a man who didn't love her. Rachel suffered because she was unable to conceive but her sister could. Jacob suffered because Laban took advantage of him and he had to work for fourteen years.

You may be questioning why God didn't intervene. Why didn't He prevent all this suffering? Why did He allow Leah to experience so much pain?

This is the question we ask God concerning all types of suffering. Why does it exist in the presence of a God who's supposed to be a loving, compassionate, and kind Father? If He loves us, wouldn't He intervene? Wouldn't He put an end to our suffering completely? Sometimes it feels like God doesn't love us at all.

Although God allows suffering, that doesn't diminish who He is. Suffering does not nullify God's nature. He remains loving, kind, and a good Father. The existence of suffering requires us to reframe our understanding of it.

What if God allows the suffering for a greater good? I can already hear your responses through my computer screen. Although you may be tempted to close the book at this juncture, hear me out. What if I hadn't suffered? I never would've started a blog, started a podcast, or written the book you're reading. In allowing me to suffer, God was focusing on the greater good that encompassed you. Suffering has a purpose. God sovereignly uses suffering for many reasons, one of them being to communicate who He is to all humanity.

God is and will always be the definition of love; suffering can't change that fact. Suffering is an unfortunate by-product of sin that entered the world when Adam and Eve ate forbidden fruit from the Tree of the Knowledge of Good and Evil.

Although suffering is a result of the sin in this world, not all suffering is a direct result of specific sin. All of us will experience suffering, but the good news is, suffering is temporary. God has promised that it will not last forever (see Rom. 8:18).

> **God sovereignly uses suffering for many reasons, one of them being to communicate who He is to all humanity.**

Even though Leah suffered, God blessed her with a fertile womb through which He would bless all humankind. We see this in Genesis 29:31 (NKJV): *"When the Lord saw that Leah was not loved, he opened her womb, but Rachel was barren."* God, in His sovereignty, was gracious to Leah. He opened her womb, and from it came the fulfillment of the Abrahamic promise. This is the promise God gave Abraham when He said, *"All peoples on earth will be blessed through you"* (Gen. 12:3). In the midst of the lying, dysfunction, jealousy, favoritism, and polygamy, God brought His purpose to perfect fruition. In the birth of Leah's children we see the spiritual transformation she went through in her relationship with God.

Reuben was her firstborn, and his name meant "behold a son." After his birth Leah said, *"It is because the Lord has seen my misery. Surely my husband will love me now"* (Gen. 29:32). Simeon was her second-born son, and his name most likely meant "one who hears." After his birth she said, *"Because the Lord heard that I am not loved, he gave me this one too"* (v. 33). Here Leah acknowledged that it was God who opened her womb, but she was still fixated on the fact that she was unloved by Jacob. Levi was her third son, and his name meant "attached." After his birth she said, *"Now at last my husband will become attached to me because I have borne him three sons"* (v. 34). Scripture doesn't give us the length of time that lapsed between Leah's pregnancies, but each day she existed in a loveless marriage must have felt unbearable for her.

Judah was her fourth son, and his name meant "praise." After his birth we see a change in Leah. Instead of focusing on finagling a way for Jacob to love her, she focused on God. She said, *"This time I will praise the Lord"* (v. 35). Although Leah desperately wanted a loving and devoted husband, it appears she found something greater—contentment.

Leah modeled a response we all can adopt. She didn't dismiss or deny her pain. She acknowledged it while also finding a reason to rejoice. Yes, father wounds are difficult, painful, and unfair, but in the midst of our pain, can we find any reason to praise God? The likelihood is that God has balanced our sorrow with blessing; we just have to be open to Him showing it to us.

God's Blessings amid Suffering

When I reflected on my life, I found an abundance of reasons to praise God. In spite of my father's absence, God placed father figures in my life. One of those men was my uncle/cousin, Raymond. Biologically, he was my second cousin, but he was raised as my mother's brother (it's complicated).

Throughout my life, he modeled what it meant to be a man, husband, and father. From him I learned masculinity can be tough and no-nonsense while still embracing a tender heart. He stepped in where my father didn't, escorting me in a cotillion, helping me purchase my first car, paying for my gas until I got on my feet as a young adult, and giving me countless nuggets of wisdom along the way.

Before Raymond died, God granted me a tender moment to say thank you to him for being like a father to me. With a quivering voice and eyes filled to the brim with tears, I expressed my sincere gratitude for his presence in my life. I will forever remember my uncle/cousin. He embraced me in ways I didn't know I needed. For a little girl raised in a single-parent household, his presence was priceless. In many ways, our relationship became a semblance of the one I longed to have with my own father. I know his presence in my life was the divine intervention of God.

God also enabled my mother to provide for our little family of two. All of my needs were met and many of my wants. We didn't live in poverty as the statistics said we were likely to do. She was able to take care of me and somehow attend my games, take me on vacations with friends, and allow me to participate in a ton of extracurricular activities. I don't know how she did it, but she did. That was yet another blessing from God.

I'm most amazed by the fact that God has blessed me with a family. I wasn't equipped to make a marriage work when I got married. Even though my husband and I had a lengthy period of premarital counseling, we still had monumental hurdles to overcome. (But God . . .)

As I write this, my husband and I are approaching our nineteenth wedding anniversary and I still love and like the man I'm married to. God has somehow made all the drama between us a beautiful display of His power in the lives of flawed people. Our marriage is not a fairy tale, and I don't even want that anymore. Fairy tales aren't real. Instead of fixating on the fairy tale, I've learned to focus on God's intended purpose for the institution of marriage. God's intention is that marriage be a representation of Christ's relationship with the church.

His relationship with us is not a fairy tale. On the contrary, it's the story of how a sinless God clothed Himself in flesh and came to earth for a disobedient and sinful people. He did this knowing we would deny, dismiss, and reject Him repeatedly, and then He died on our behalf. He willingly took the shorter end of the stick, demonstrating how husbands everywhere should treat their wives. This is the type of marriage I desire. The man lays down his life for the woman and the woman humbly submits to the man, thus reflecting what a relationship with Christ should embody. This is not a fairy tale but a beautiful depiction of love in a marriage.

As I've worked through an abundance of issues, I'm grateful to say I've seen my husband lay his life down for me. Although neither one of us grew up in a household with a father or seeing a marriage at work, God has enabled us to have a family. As with any marriage, we have our "intense times of fellowship," but we're unified in working to honor God with our marriage.

I could go on, but you get the point. In this life God balances our valleys with mountaintop experiences. We need the joy and sorrow, disappointment and excitement, hardship and seasons of ease. God weaves them together masterfully to communicate who He is to humanity.

Your story may not look like mine. Maybe God blessed you with a kind stepfather, a concerned neighbor, or a really good friend. Know that the people God placed in your life to help you process your pain are not there by coincidence. I believe the sovereign God of the entire universe intentionally placed them in your life because of His great love for you.

In all of our lives, no matter the pain we have suffered, there's always a reason to praise the Lord. God takes our pain and makes it beautiful, just as it says in Isaiah 61:1–3: *"The Spirit of the Sovereign Lord is on me because the Lord has anointed me . . . to bestow on them a crown of beauty instead of ashes, the oil of joy instead of mourning, and a garment of praise instead of a spirit of despair."*

You may be saying, "I don't see any blessings in my life. That's great for you, Kia, but that's not my story! I didn't have any father figures. I did grow up in poverty. I did become a teenage mother. I was abused. I experimented with drugs and alcohol, and my marriage (or marriages) fell completely apart. I'm glad that you can see mountaintops among your valleys, but I don't see anything at all to be happy about. I don't have a reason to praise God, because my entire life has been negatively impacted by my father wounds."

If that's you, first let me say, I'm so sorry for the pain you experienced. I'm sorry for the ways your father wounds have impacted your life. What happened to you is not your fault. You deserved to be loved and cared for.

I want you to know that the pain you suffered isn't a barometer for God's love for you. His love remains constant. Just as it says in Romans 8:38–39, *"For I am convinced that neither death nor life, neither angels nor demons, neither the present nor the future, nor any powers, neither height nor depth, nor anything else in all creation, will be able to separate us from the love of God that is in Christ Jesus our Lord."*

The mere fact that you're reading this book is evidence of His lavish love for you. It's not happenstance that you picked up this book. It's not a coincidence that I wrote it. I believe God had you in mind every step of the way.

The reality is, no matter how painfully difficult life can be, we're still here to experience it all. We can praise God for life itself even if it's hard. Even if our father wounds have made our lives tough, we can celebrate the fact that we have another opportunity to rise above our circumstances, thank God for His goodness, and rejoice at His ability to do immeasurably more than we could ask or imagine for each of us (see Eph. 3:20).

No matter what our story is, God is in the business of exchanging our father wounds for His great love. We see this in the life of Leah because God made her the mother of Judah, from whom the Savior of the world descended. God could've opted to allow Rachel to be Judah's mother—she was Jacob's first choice—but He chose Leah to birth him instead. He balanced Leah's sorrow with joy.

In Genesis 29:35, Leah reached the place we all must come to in life—the place where we stop chasing everyone and everything that's not chasing us back and pursue a relationship with the One who is, God our heavenly Father. He is the loving God who created our innermost being and knit us together in our mother's womb (see Ps. 139:13). He is the God whose love is so steadfast and audacious that He would send His only begotten Son to die a lonely, gruesome death on a cross so that we might have unlimited access to Him (see John 3:16). He is the God who is so concerned about women with father wounds that He mentions the fatherless forty-five times in the Bible.

Sis, I believe He did this with you in mind. He wanted you to know that never have you ever been forgotten. He has always seen you and the pain you suffered. He has always been concerned for you.

God's View of Good—and Ours

The fact that God allows women to experience father wounds doesn't change His attributes. Although it's difficult for us to perceive Him as a good, loving, and compassionate Father when He allows painful things in our lives, that doesn't change His nature; His nature doesn't change.

It took me decades to understand this, and consequently I spent many years angry with God. I thought He was unfair because He allowed me to grow up without my father. Now I can quote Romans 8:28 and see the tangible ways this verse has manifested in my life: *"And we know that in all things God works for the good of those who love him, who have been called according to his purpose."*

The Greek word for *good* is *agathós*, and it describes what originates from God and is empowered by Him. This means that what God sees as good may differ from our perspective. What God views as good is good whether we think it is or not. God has an infinite and eternal view of good, and our view has a tendency to be finite and carnal. We often see good from our fleshly perspectives. What feels good, appeals to our five senses, and is perceived as good by others is what we generally think of as good.

God's idea of good, however, doesn't have to fit into our limited parameters. His view of good encompasses pain. He's able to take our pain and use it to heal brokenness, mend relationships, and grow us in Christlike character.

I love how Lisa Whittle describes good in her book *The Hard Good*. She says,

> And what may be the most important thing to note from that quotable in Romans 8: "All things work together for good" (v. 28 KJV): the most missed word in the verse is "together," and it's the most important. It does not say that all things work out. It says all things work together. This means that there will be missteps, disappointments, losses, and things that fall through along the way. Not everything in this world will work out for us. But the hard things will work together for good for those who love God and desire to be usable for His kingdom.[4]

God uses all things to fulfill His purposes in the earth; this includes our pain. In my own life, He has used the pain of my father wounds to encourage the hearts of other women like me.

Had I grown up with my ideal father, I wouldn't have started a blog several years ago, and I definitely wouldn't be writing this book. God knew the pain I had to experience in order to fulfill my God-ordained destiny on the earth.

The Story of Joseph

This reminds me of another person in the Old Testament. In the book of Genesis, Joseph was the second-youngest son of Jacob. He had previously been the only son born to Rachel, and as a result he was overtly favored by Jacob. This made his brothers very jealous, and when Joseph was seventeen, they threw him in a cistern and sold him into slavery to the Ishmaelites. From there he was purchased by the Egyptians, falsely imprisoned, and forgotten for thirteen years of his life (Gen. 37–39).

Joseph had ample opportunities to dwell on the pain he suffered. He may have reasoned how unfair his lot in life had been. Joseph may have even uttered a few times, "Why me?" He had been thrust into a life he didn't choose for himself. He was suffering because of pain inflicted on him by his family members.

Maybe he expected his brothers to love and protect him unconditionally, but he experienced betrayal instead. Joseph was wounded, and the pain he endured lasted for years. Every time he thought of his plight in life, he may have been tempted to rehearse a familiar chorus of anger, sorrow, and unforgiveness. Despite the obvious challenges he faced, Scripture reminds us of an encouraging truth in Genesis 39:20–21: *"But while Joseph was there in the prison, the Lord was with him; he showed him kindness and granted him favor in the eyes of the prison warden."*

"*The* Lord *was with Joseph*" occurs four times in Genesis 39, and it provides a glimmer of hope in Joseph's challenging circumstance. Even though life was unfair and painful, the omniscient, omnipotent, and omnipresent God was with Joseph. His presence continued to comfort Joseph in the midst of his pain.

This speaks of the overwhelming love of God. As Joseph weathered his difficulties, he was not abandoned. God was not absent. While Joseph grieved what had been lost, God lavishly loved him. And when Joseph's unfair trial ended and he was exalted to second-in-command to Pharaoh, his wounds were overshadowed by God's continuous love. Joseph was able to see how the pain God allowed him to experience ultimately benefited him and others: "*You intended to harm me, but God intended it for good to accomplish what is now being done, the saving of many lives*" (Gen. 50:20).

Nestled in the middle of this verse we see the word *good* again. God took Joseph's betrayal, slavery, and false imprisonment and worked it all together for good. Joseph realized that even though God allowed him to suffer unfair treatment and overwhelming pain for years, a greater plan was at work. Had Joseph not been sold into slavery and falsely imprisoned, he wouldn't have been in the position to save the lives of many, including his family.

The same is true for you. God is able to take all the pain you've experienced and work it together for your ultimate good. He has a purpose for your pain. Often He uses our painful stories as the healing balm He applies to the wounds of others.

My Story

While I was suffering, I wasn't concerned with my purpose or God's plan. I was concerned with my pain. I pursued my father for years before I realized he had an alcohol addiction. He struggled with this disease well into my adult life. It impacted several areas of my life and his, and the consequences were devastating, as you can imagine. One of those consequences was a strained relationship with me.

My dad missed several milestones in my life. He missed my first and last day of elementary, middle, and high school (not to mention all the days in between). He never went to an awards program. He never attended a volleyball game or a track meet. He didn't attend any of my grade school graduations. He never saw me perform in a play. He never saw me all dressed up for prom. He didn't see me off for college. He missed much of my childhood and adolescence.

Consequently, I was bitter, angry, and frustrated about his absence in my life. It took me years to process my pain and forgive him. Even while I was pursuing a relationship with him, forgiveness was a struggle for me. I found myself cycling through the same emotions over and over. I would feel free and then somehow find myself entangled in unforgiveness again. There would be a new offense on top of the old offense I was already trying to forgive, and the cycle would start all over. To say that I struggled is an understatement.

I was tempted to give up on the relationship many times. I felt like I was constantly being taken advantage of. He messed up and I came in to save him, desperately hoping the next time would be different. There were times when I found myself helping my father when I needed him to be a father for me. Honestly, if it wasn't for God compelling me to love my dad, I wouldn't have been able to do it.

In saying this, I recommend that father-wounded daughters seek wise, sound, professional counseling before engaging with their fathers. It can be difficult and complicated, especially if your father has an addiction. In my case, I relied on the Spirit of God. He led me every step of the way, and I had confidence that I was doing what God required of me. God enabled me to love my father out of the abundant love He had given me. It was one of the most challenging things I've ever done, but I would do it all over again because I've seen God's power in my obedience.

God's power has changed both me and my dad. As I learned to love the man my father was and stopped attempting to make him who I wanted him to be, God's supernatural power transformed my heart. He showed me what it means to have the type of love we see in 1 Corinthians 13:4–8: *"Love is patient, love is kind. It does not envy, it does not boast, it is not proud. It does not dishonor others, it is not self-seeking, it is not easily angered, it keeps no record of wrongs. Love does not delight in evil but rejoices with the truth. It always protects, always trusts, always hopes, always perseveres. Love never fails."*

Before I began to love my father without expectation, I thought I had a corner on the 1 Corinthians 13 type of love. I treated people right and did my best to love my neighbor. I was a good person. But loving people when it's easy to love them isn't all we're called to do. We are also to love people when it's downright hard to do. Loving in this way requires acknowledging how someone didn't, doesn't, and can't love you, and deciding, *I'm going to choose to love them anyway.* This love is supernatural and unexplainable, and it goes against what feels natural. This love is a choice.

I couldn't fake or buy this love. Only a holy God could cultivate this love in me over time with my every act of obedience. Call your father today. Go and visit him. Help him resolve this problem. Serve him. Write him a letter. Pay for his bill. Forgive him. Help him in the way God has helped you: unconditionally, faithfully, freely, and sacrificially. With each prompting from the Holy Spirit, God is saying, "This is how I love humanity—with no strings attached. This is how I love you. This is how I love your father."

We're not deserving of His love. We can't earn it, nor do we always appreciate and recognize the difference His love makes in our lives. His love changes us.

I recognized this when my dad had a close encounter with death. Unexpectedly, I received a phone call on a Friday afternoon. It was my dad's landlord saying there had been an incident at the residence where he lived. Immediately, I panicked. She proceeded to describe the events as she watched them take place in real time on the video surveillance. She described my father's close call with death and then said, "He could have died."

Inadvertently, I held my breath as fear completely gripped my heart. At that moment I was keenly aware that if my father had lost his life that day, I would've been devastated. I wouldn't have been concerned about the events he missed, or the things he did or didn't do. I wouldn't have been bitter about his absence in my adolescence. I would've felt the sting of losing my biological father. No matter who he was and what he'd done, I would've been devastated.

As I later reflected on that phone call, it dawned on me that God had changed my heart. There was a time in my life when bitterness and anger held my heart hostage and I wasn't concerned about my father's well-being. God replaced all that darkness with an unconditional love that didn't want anything in return. In that moment I recognized that no matter how my dad has struggled in this life, I will only get one father. His absence will be a tremendous loss for me and my family.

God spared his life that day, and He taught me the value of loving without expectation while trusting Him to do the rest. God may not require you to be a part of your father's life in the same way He asked of me. Loving your dad may mean forgiving him. It may mean calling him. It may mean allowing him to meet his grandkids. Loving your father may look like serving him in some way. I'm convinced whatever God has asked you to do in the name of extending 1 Corinthians 13 love to your father is for your good and will be worth it.

A few weeks ago, I experienced another "worth it" moment. My editor advised me to secure my father's permission to share sensitive details about his life. He had already given me his verbal permission, but I wanted him to hear the exact words I penned on paper. As a result, I hopped on a plane and traveled eight hundred miles to my hometown one weekend in October. It was a warm Saturday evening when I drove to my dad's residence to pick him up.

He came out wearing a freshly dry-cleaned suit, a pin-striped shirt, and shined dress shoes. He was clean-shaven, and his cologne greeted me before he did. His face beamed with joy and was matched only by his larger-than-life grin. Then he puffed out his chest as he introduced me to his roommates, "This is my daughter." I was glad to meet the people in my dad's life, but was even more grateful to see the pride with which my father introduced me to his friends.

As we drove to a Mexican restaurant, the magnitude of what I was about to do hadn't sunk in yet. I didn't feel nervous about reading my book. There were no butterflies floating around my stomach.

At our table in the restaurant, I pulled out my pink laptop and sat it next to the chips and salsa, connected to Wi-Fi, and opened my document. That's when it happened. *Are you really ready to do this?* I questioned myself. Up until this point, I mostly kept things light between my father and me. There was that one time when I told him about my blog, but this was different. This time I would be publishing a book and telling the whole world my father struggled with an alcohol addiction. I contemplated not going through with it, but I had come too far to turn back now. The only way to the other side of this moment was to go through it.

I began to read, intentionally keeping my eyes on the computer screen so I wouldn't have to make eye contact with him. It was difficult and awkward on many levels. Although I'd read the words in the chapter you're reading countless times, they sounded different as I read them to my father. More vulnerable. More heavy. More painful. More real.

Somehow, I mustered up the courage to lift my eyes from the computer screen. "Are you okay with what I just said?" I timidly asked.

"Sure," he said with his thick Haitian accent. "That is the way it happened." Then he continued munching on a tortilla chip.

I kept reading until I'd shared all the sections that pertained to him. Then I paused before asking him what he thought one last time. Graciously, he told me everything I shared was okay. Then out of nowhere he said, "I owe you and your mother an apology." His voice went up an octave and began to tremble as Texas-sized tears dripped down his face. "I asked God to take the alcohol away from me because it destroyed my life." Then he started to sob.

I wasn't ready for this moment. I was a forty-two-year-old woman staring as my almost seventy-year-old father grieved for the unforgiving consequences of alcoholism. And in that moment I was thankful that my heart was genuinely overflowing with compassion. I was keenly aware that my father had been given a gift that he was now sharing with me: a repentant heart.

My father, who had at this point been sober for more than a year, was truly sorrowful for his sins. He was wholeheartedly saying, "I'm sorry for the pain I caused you." I not only accepted his apology but also recognized the commonality between us.

Although I have never struggled with alcohol, I have struggled with sin. A lot. I was no different from him. My sin was just a little easier to conceal. "It's okay, Dad," I responded. "Everybody has something we struggle with."

Y'all, God was working as we sat at that Mexican restaurant. I saw Him in my father's repentance. I saw Him in the kindness that flowed from my heart. I saw Him in the love my father and I shared and the beautiful story He had written. Had I never leaned into loving my father in the way God was urging me to, I would've missed this "worth it" moment.

Your Story

Sis, I know what I know. Showing 1 Corinthians 13 love to a father who didn't father you doesn't make sense. Society would say you're justified in treating your father badly because of your father wounds: "Give him a dose of his own medicine. Ignore him. Hate him. Dismiss him. Deny him. Hurt him. Give him what he deserves." You'd be encouraged to cut him out of your life completely, but God doesn't say this. He says, *"So in everything, do to others what you would have them do to you, for this sums up the Law and the Prophets"* (Matt. 7:12).

Yes, it feels unnatural to extend love to the man who didn't father you, but trust God, your heavenly Father. His ways are not like our ways. In doing so you'll overcome your father wounds and show the love of Christ Jesus to your father, who may not experience this type of love anywhere else.

This is how we overcome, incrementally. Step. By. Challenging. Step. This is not a quick and speedy process. With each act of obedience, as we do what God is asking us to do as it relates to our fathers, God does surgery on our hearts. He breaks the hold our father wounds have on our lives. This is what He did in my life. One day I realized I was no longer handcuffed to my wounds anymore.

In saying this, I want you to know I still have a good cry every now and then. I can't predict when the tears will flow down my cheeks, but they do continue to fall. Sometimes it happens when I see that dad in Target lovingly holding his little girl. Sometimes it occurs when a woman describes the tender actions of her father.

When it does, I give myself permission to grieve. I'm not ashamed that I still cry, nor do I feel like I should be done crying. For me, grieving is part of the process of healing, and it may continue until the day I see my Savior face-to-face. I grieve the things I know I'll never experience. I grieve the tremendous loss. I grieve the pain. But my grief does not mean I have not overcome.

I have overcome because grief doesn't have a hold on me. I'm no longer bound to my pain—imprisoned by the past and unable to move forward. I grieve, but not as one who has no hope (see 1 Thess. 4:13). I know hope because I know God who is my hope, as it says in Romans 15:13: *"May the God of hope fill you with all joy and peace as you trust in him, so that you may overflow with hope by the power of the Holy Spirit."*

Sis, it's okay to cry. Exchanging our pain for God's perfect love is no walk in the park and it doesn't happen overnight, but it can happen. I'm reminded of this in one of my favorite verses, Philippians 1:6: *"Being confident of this, that he who began a good work in you will carry it on to completion until the day of Christ Jesus."* God will finish the good work of exchanging your pain for His perfect love. That is a promise we can count on.

This truth was reiterated for me in Psalm 147:3, *"He heals the brokenhearted and binds up their wounds."* Although this

Scripture is specifically referring to the exiles of Israel, I believe these words are applicable to women with father wounds. In this verse God is reminding us that our pain is not beyond His tremendous power. He is the Great Physician, able to reach into our past and heal our soul.

The Scripture says "He heals," meaning this healing is ongoing. It is not a onetime deal but rather a supernatural act that can occur over and over in the life of the brokenhearted. For as much and as long as we need healing, God's compassionate care is available to us.

> In God we are already overcomers, and we can choose to exchange insecurity for security, fear for faith, despair for hope, and wounds for the lavish love of our heavenly Father.

The Hebrew meaning for the word "brokenhearted" is defined as the inner man: encompassing the mind, will, and emotions. God is capable of healing our unseen places. He not only heals the soul of the broken, but He also binds up our wounds.

This is my favorite part of this Scripture because the word "wounds" is plural. This means it does not matter how many wounds we identify in our lives, whether they are physical, mental, or emotional, God is able to heal them all.

He takes the time to tenderly bandage the wounded places in our souls so that we can be made whole. One day the sting of father wounds will be gone completely. God will wipe away every tear from our eyes once and for all (see Rev. 21:4). This is a promise we have and an eternal hope found only in God our heavenly Father.

Sis, there is hope for you and me. Hope to be fully healed. Hope to be secure. Hope to be free—completely free. Hope to be satisfied with the love of God alone. Hope to overcome all our father wounds. In God we are already overcomers, and we can choose to exchange insecurity for security, fear for faith, despair for hope, and wounds for the perfect love of our heavenly Father.

Practical Ways to Make Peace with the Present

- Answer the small group discussion questions.
- Express your feelings in a journal.
- Discuss your emotions with a trusted friend.
- Join a support group.
- Pray to God about your pain.

Questions for Reflection

1. Read and memorize 2 Corinthians 5:7; Romans 8:15; 1 John 3:1; and Psalm 68:5.
2. How did your parents meet?
3. What type of upbringing did your mother have? Was she fathered?
4. What type of upbringing did your father have? Was he fathered?
5. How might God be leading you to offer your parents grace?
6. In what ways might you be able to show love to your father?

7. Where do you see God's blessings in the midst of difficulty as it relates to your father wounds?

8. Has the love of God changed your heart as it relates to your father? How might God desire to change your heart toward your dad?

CONSIDERING CHRIST

Exchanging father wounds for the love of God the Father isn't possible without a relationship with Jesus Christ. He's the One who makes forgiveness, healing, peace, courage, love, hope, and purity possible.

My relationship with Christ has truly changed my life for the better and for good. This doesn't mean I don't experience hardships or challenges. It simply means I go through my difficulties relying on the strength and power of the living God.

If you're interested in exchanging your father wounds for the love of God the Father, beginning a relationship with Jesus Christ is a prerequisite step you must take. This decision has completely changed my life, and I can't think of a better decision anyone could make.

For making this commitment, God has given us some simple steps in His Word. You need only a willing heart. Romans 10:8–13 says,

The word is near you; it is in your mouth and in your heart, that is, the message concerning faith that we proclaim: If you declare with your mouth, "Jesus is Lord," and believe in your heart that

God raised Him from the dead, you will be saved. For it is with your heart that you believe and are justified, and it is with your mouth that you profess your faith and are saved. As Scripture says, "Anyone who believes in him will never be put to shame." For there is no difference between Jew and Gentile—the same Lord is Lord of all and richly blesses all who call on him, or, "Everyone who calls on the name of the Lord will be saved."

If you desire to experience the gift of salvation today, I'll lead you through the simple prayer below. Sis, imagine that I'm right there with you, holding your hand and cheering you on as you recite these words.

Dear Lord,

Thank You for the gift of salvation. I believe that You died on a cross for my sins and that God raised You up from the dead. I believe that in Your resurrection You conquered sin and death. As a result, I can know salvation, hope, healing, forgiveness, courage, love, validation, security, peace, and so much more in You. I confess with my mouth that Jesus is Lord, and I ask You to come and live in my heart. Thank You that You have not abandoned me, nor have You ever left me. Thank You that You are my heavenly Father.

In Jesus's name, amen.

If you prayed this prayer, that's it! Welcome to the Christian faith. Salvation is immediate; however, the process of becoming like Christ takes time. For this reason I'd recommend becoming a part of a growing community of believers that can support you on this new journey. If you made the decision to give your life to Christ, I'd be honored if you would share that with me so that I can pray for you as you begin your new journey.

ACKNOWLEDGMENTS

My Heavenly Father

I would be remiss if I didn't acknowledge You first. If I were You, I don't think I would've ever taken a gamble on me to do anything. At best I'm inconsistent. Sometimes faithful. Often scared. Easily agitated. Prone to quit.

You know more than anyone that there's no possible way in the world I could have completed this book without Your supernatural strength. Amazingly, You know everything that I could not and would not put in the pages of this book, and yet You still desire to know and love me lavishly.

If there were no You, there would be no book, and for that I owe You my deepest gratitude. You are the sole reason I'm living and able to encourage others with the encouragement You have given me. You are my rock, my comfort, my source, my heavenly Father, and the secret sauce behind everything I do. I owe You my life.

Jeff

More than anyone, you know what it has taken for me to write this book. You have been there for my tears, rants, rage, insecurities, doubts, confusion, brokenness, sin, heartache, shame, fear, and guilt. Thank you for staying. Thank you for praying. Thank you for speaking. Thank you for remaining silent. Thank you for sacrificing, and thank you for loving me with the unconditional love of Christ.

Though I didn't have the privilege of watching my father love my mother, I have had a front-row seat to watching you love me and be an amazing father to our boys. You have walked this journey with me and given me the time, space, and grace I needed to grow up. Thank you for freeing me to write, which has played a critical role in my healing journey. Your willingness to allow me to discover my writing potential has enabled me to write this book, and for that I say thank you.

Jeffrey and Jonathan

I marvel at the fact that I get to raise you two. You give Mom so much life. Though you are my kids, I have gleaned from your wisdom and encouragement many times over. Thank you for praying for Mommy to finish this book, missing movie nights, and having sandwiches for dinner. Mommy owes you a date night to make up for the lost time. I hope that finishing this book is a reminder to you to complete what you start no matter the obstacles you face in life. You both have so much potential, and I can't wait to see what God does with your gifts and talents.

Mom

I can only imagine how tough it was to be a single mother raising me. I know I gave you many reasons to stay on your knees. Thank you for never giving up, working inside and outside the home, volunteering at my school, driving me EVERYWHERE, exposing me to so much, and teaching me how to pray. I know it was difficult when I began to pursue a relationship with my father, and I thank you for giving me the space to do it. This book is a by-product of your willingness to let me find my own way.

Dad

Thank you for giving me the freedom to tell this story. It is not easy to share our hard truth with the world, but you gave me permission to do so. Because of you, many will know God's redemptive power. Although our relationship has not been ideal, I believe God has made it beautiful.

Aunt Gloria

You have always loved me more like a daughter than a niece. Thank you for helping to raise me and providing support for my mom as a single parent.

Christina

Thanks for listening to me talk about this book for the duration of our friendship. You never gave up on the book even though I did many times. Thank you for talking me off the wall on numerous occasions and reminding me that there was a woman attached to my words. Your encouragement has been invaluable.

Maya

Thank you for encouraging me to start a blog seven years ago. You saw past my pain and focused on my purpose. Your words helped me keep going after a tremendous setback.

Revell Books

Andrea, thank you for asking Natasha to e-introduce you to me. I know our meeting was providential. Thank you for not only initiating the meeting but also doing your homework. The day I met with you was the encouragement I needed to not give up on this twenty-year-old book idea.

Wendy, thank you for responding to all my emails with grace

and patience. Sarah, thanks for taking care of ALL my requests! Eileen, thank you for listening to my BIG ideas and allocating funds so I can make them happen. Barb, thank you for being a follower of Christ first and an editor second. Christi, thank you for your attention to detail and thoughtful comments. The entire Revell team, thank you for getting behind this book project. You were my first choice and God's best for this book.

Jevon

Thank you for being my friend before you were my literary agent. You patiently waited on me and then you helped me along the way. I'm so grateful that you said the words, "I would love to represent you." It was definitely one of the best decisions I've made in my writing career. I can't wait to work on more book projects with you!

Entrusted Women

Natasha, thanks for the e-introduction! Tasha, thank you for being my friend and my launch team manager. Ariane, thank you for managing EVERYTHING! Kia G., thank you for working with my creative control tendencies and making me look FABULOUS on the internet. Najah, thank you for being the friend I didn't know I needed and the counselor I don't have to pay for. Nicole, thank you for being a friend while I processed my wounds.

And to every Entrusted Woman, you are the sisterhood I never knew I needed. Serving you changed me and literally made it possible for me to get a book deal. I hope I get to serve you for the rest of my days. In a sense, you all are a part of my destiny. I'm grateful for everything and anything you have done for me. Thank you for believing, praying, encouraging, promoting, and helping me get the word out about this book. I want you to know I appreciate it all, and I can't wait till it's your turn and I get to say, "I see you, sis!"

NOTES

Chapter 1 Sounding the Alarm

1. Denna Babul and Karin Luise, *The Fatherless Daughter Project* (New York: Avery, 2016), xx.

Chapter 2 Diagnosing the Obvious

1. Robert S. McGee, *The Search for Significance* (Nashville: Thomas Nelson, 2003), 29.
2. James Dobson, *Bringing Up Girls* (Wheaton: Tyndale House, 2018), 87.

Chapter 3 Interrogating the Past

1. John and Stasi Eldredge, *Captivating: Unveiling the Mystery of a Woman's Soul*, rev. ed. (Nashville: Thomas Nelson, 2008), 46.
2. U.S. Census Bureau, "Living Arrangements of Children under 18 Years Old: 1960 to Present," Washington, DC: U.S. Census Bureau, 2021, https://cdn2 .hubspot.net/hubfs/135704/NFIFatherAbsenceInfoGraphic071118.pdf.
3. H. Norman Wright, *Always Daddy's Girl: Understanding Your Father's Impact on Who You Are* (Ventura, CA: Regal Books, 2001), 41.
4. Mark Gungor, *Laugh Your Way to a Better Marriage* (New York: Atria, 2009).
5. Wright, *Always Daddy's Girl*, 43.

Chapter 4 Wrestling with the Real

1. Bill Gillham, *Lifetime Guarantee: Making Your Christian Life Work and What to Do When It Doesn't* (Eugene, Oregon: Harvest House, 1993), 105.
2. Wright, *Always Daddy's Girl*, 35.

Chapter 5 Creating My Ideal

1. Henry Cloud and John Townsend, *Boundaries: When to Say Yes, How to Say No to Take Control of Your Life* (Grand Rapids: Zondervan, 1992), 29.

Chapter 6 Forgiving the Unpardonable

1. Lysa TerKeurst, *Forgiving What You Can't Forget* (Nashville: Thomas Nelson, 2020), 28.

2. Charles L. Whitfield, *Healing the Child Within: Discovery and Recovery for Adult Children of Dysfunctional Families* (Deerfield, FL: Health Communications, Inc., 2006), 89.

3. TerKeurst, *Forgiving What You Can't Forget*, 29.

Chapter 7 Overcoming the Pain

1. Andy Stanley, "Re-Assembly Required: A Beginner's Guide to Repairing Broken Relationships," Buckhead Church, October 31, 2021.

Chapter 8 Believing in the Impossible

1. Matthew Brown, "Father's Faith: Perceptions of God May Stem from Dad–Child Relationships," Culture, *Washington Times*, June 15, 2013.

2. *Re:New: Freedom to Experience the Christian Life as God Intended*, rev. ed. (Alpharetta, GA: North Point Ministries, Inc., 2017), 66.

3. John Gill, "Commentaries Genesis 16:7," Biblehub.com., retrieved October 16, 2021, https://biblehub.com/commentaries/genesis/16-7.htm.

4. U.S. Census Bureau, "The Father Absence Crisis in America," infographic, 2021, National Fatherhood Initiative, https://cdn2.hubspot.net/hubfs/135704/NFIFatherAbsenceInfoGraphic071118.pdf.

Chapter 9 Making Peace with the Present

1. T. D. Jakes, *He Motions: Strength for Men, Solutions for Women*, reprint ed. (New York: Berkley, 2012), 200.

2. Stephen Arterburn, *The Secrets Men Keep* (Nashville: Thomas Nelson, 2007), 53.

3. U.S. Census Bureau, "Living Arrangements."

4. Lisa Whittle, *The Hard Good* (Nashville: W Publishing Group, 2021), xvi.

Kia Stephens is the founder of Entrusted Women, which she created to equip Christian women communicators of color. A contributing writer for iBelieve.com, Beloved Women, Proverbs 31 Ministries, and Crosswalk, she is a recurring speaker at She Speaks, the Beloved Women's Conference, and the Entrusted Women's Conference. Kia's writing has been featured on (in)courage and Ann Voskamp's blog. She has also been a featured guest on the *Proverbs 31 Ministries Podcast, Chrystal's Chronicles* with Chrystal Evans Hurst, *Better Together* with Barb Roose, and *The Dream of You Podcast* with Jo Saxton. When she is not writing or serving women, she enjoys spending quality time with her family and friends. You can learn more about Kia at www.kiastephens.com.

Connect with
KIA STEPHENS

Find Kia online for more *Overcoming Father Wounds* resources, including a video Bible study. To access additional video content for each chapter, visit https://www.kiastephens.com/books/.

Listen in to Kia's podcast or sign up for her email list for encouragement, healing, and practical wisdom on a regular basis.